CW01313935

Elven Geomancy:

An Ancient Oracle of the Elfin Peoples for Divination and Spell Casting

The Silver Elves

Copyright © 2017 The Silver Elves, Michael J Love and Martha C. Love

All rights reserved.

Cover image is from photo taken at Todaiji Temple, Nara, Japan, by Silver Flame of Zardoa standing in front of the statue of Binzuru (Pindola Bharadvaja), one of the original four arhats of early Indian Buddhism, known for his magical healing and his mastery of occult and psychic powers.

ISBN-13: 978-1974344468

ISBN-10: 1974344460

Printed in the United States of America by CreateSpace

Without limiting the rights under the copyright reserved above, no part of this publication may be reproduced, stored in or introduced into a retrieval system, or transmitted in any form or by any means (electronic, mechanical, by photocopying, recording or otherwise) without the prior written permission of the copyright owner and the publisher of the book.

Dedication

We dedicate this book to all our elven brothers and sisters.

"Among some elves, the weavers of the Fates are viewed as an ancient witch known as the Necromancer who carries a crystal ball, removes disused cobwebs with her broom and rules the Past. The Present is dominated by a bald middle aged male who carries a staff and does martial arts katas while reciting spells. He is known as the Dancer. And the Future is created by an androgynous child who plays with figures in a sand box imagining the future into being. No one knows this one's name, although some call Hir Starlight."

—The Silver Elves

Table of Contents

Introduction

Elven Geomancy differs quite a bit from the traditional geomancy that was used by the ancients and the people of the Renaissance and Middle Ages. That form of geomancy was at one time rather widely known and popular among diviners, although it has, for the most part, fallen out of use today. If you wish to know about that method of geomancy we highly recommend Israel Regardie's small but informative book *A Practical Guide to Geomantic Divination.* The primary difference between that form of geomancy and elven geomancy is that it had sixteen possible outcomes that would arrange in a series of twelve, which then combined to produce three more figures to give you your answer. Elven geomancy has 128 possible outcomes that give a reply of a series of seven (like the seven pointed star of the elves) oracles as your response. These seven oracles show the step by step process or movement toward the realization of your question.

We make no claim that our elven way is superior to the way of the ancients. Merely that it is different and beloved by these elves. You may, as always, decide for your own s'elf which one, if either, you prefer or if you like both methods. The elven method draws from a wider range of possible outcomes and yet is simpler in form. However, the ancient method is strongly associated with astrology and the astrological houses and so for astrologers it may be a better or more interesting method or at least one that draws on information with which they are already knowledgeable. We are elven astrologers, so we understand the other method, but we still prefer our own for our method is also a means of creating magical elfin spells to help bring about our wishes.

Getting the Oracles, Drawing the Grandparents

In traditional geomancy, one makes a random series of dots on a piece of paper or in the sand (actually the earliest form had to do with finding a series of random dots, perhaps raindrops or even water cast after washing one's hands, in the desert sand). In that form, the diviner makes sixteen rows of dots quickly and without thinking about it. If you used this technique in the elven method, you would make four sets of seven rows of dots. That would be seven rows for each of what are known as the four grandparents.

You then count up the dots and if the line has an even number of dots it is an O (or in the old method two X's) and if it has an odd number it is written down as an X.

For our own part, these elves prefer to use a die. Throwing one die seven times and putting down the results from the bottom up, thus creating what we call your first grandparent. You do this three more times, which is to say, you create four figures in all by this process. These are the grandparents. It doesn't really matter what die you use as long as it has an equal number of possibilities for odd and even. It could be a six sided die or a twenty sided die, as gamers sometimes use.

Of course, you could also have equal sized white and a black stones in a bag, or a series of white or black stones (or any color for that matter) and reach in and take one out, using black (let's say) for even and white for odd or vice versa. You would put the stone back in the bag after noting it each time so there would always be an equal possibility for odd X or even O to come up. Again, you would create four figures composed of seven letters of X or O's or a combination there of.

We're sure you could think of other ways to get the figures as well. You could even figure out how to use playing cards or tarot cards, as long as the chances of getting odd or even are always equal.

The Parents

Once you have obtained the four grandparents you can now move on to the process of getting the parents. The parents come from combining the grandparents into pairs. It is up to you to decide which grandparent goes or mates with which other grandparent. The first grandparent can be combined with the second, third or fourth grandparent, and then, obviously, the other two left will combine. However, it is best if you make this choice instinctually, as randomly as possible and you may wish to choose which ones will combine before you even draw the oracle. But that is up to you.

The combination goes as follows. If the first two figures of the combined grandparents are even or O that creates an even or O figure. The same is true if both figures are odd X, this combination also creates an O or even figure. However, any combination of odd X and even O will create an odd X figure.

This is easy to understand if we consider odd or X to be 1 and even or O to be 2. If you add two 2s you get four, an even number and if you add two 1s you get 2, also an even number, but any combination of 1 and 2 will always come out 3 an odd O number.

Thus if your grandparents were the following combination:

X	**X**	**O**		
X	**O**		**X**	
O	**O**		**O**	
O	**X**	**THESE TWO BECOME THIS**		**X**
X	**O**		**X**	
O	**O**		**O**	
X	**X**		**O**	

After pairing the four grandparents, you now have two parents. When you combine these two parents you get the child, which is the final outcome and oracle for the question you asked. It is quite simple really.

It may happen that the outcome you receive is not what you had entirely hoped. And as is obvious you could recombine the grandparents and wind up with another child or outcome, or draw/cast the entire oracle series again but believe us when we tell you that it is unlikely that doing so will erase the psychological power of the first outcome. However, instead you may use the recombination of the grandparents in your magic, the mantras and mudras that come with each combination, in order to heighten the chances of a better result. See below.

Refer to Appendix B for tables that will let you easily find the chapter number for the oracles you have drawn.

Mantra

The mantras that accompany each of the oracles are written in Arvyndase (see our book *Arvyndase [SilverSpeech]: the Magical Language of the Silver Elves*) and can be strung together to form a spell to increase the magic associated with the answer you receive and may be used along with the mudra to form a sort of impromptu ritual that you can perform in order to increase the potency of what you wish to achieve. It is always possible, and is likely to be the case sometimes that the answer you received was not the one you were hoping for. You are free, of course, to put together any series and combination of mantras and mudras that you feel may increase your potentiality for success in terms of the question asked and the outcome desired. Merely recombine the grandparents and see what outcome you then get. If you like it better, use that series of mantras and mudras to subtly shift the energy. Do this magic until you achieve the result you desire.

Mudra

There are eight basic mudra hand positions that are used in this book. By placing one's hand in these positions and then following the movements as described a magical spell casting is created. When one links these movements derived from the oracle together, along with the mantras, one has a mini ritual that one can use to empower one's desires or avoid outcomes or obstacles one doesn't wish to manifest.

In moving from the end of one set of movements to the starting point of the next set, make your transition from one position to the other as efficient and elegant as possible. In making the seven movements, connect them as one movement visualizing the colors for the movements and connecting the movements between them so they become one continuous series. This, of course, will take a bit of practice.

The mudra positions and movement will involve both hands. When speaking of the mudra positions we will refer to your dominant and assisting hands. If you are right handed that will be your dominant hand and the left your assisting hand. If you are left handed the reference will be reversed. If you are ambidextrous the dominant hand will be the one with which you sign your name and the assisting hand the one that holds the paper. Or if you wish, merely choose which hand you wish to use as the dominant hand and assisting hand. It's your magic, after all.

Refer to Appendix A for photos of the eight basic hand positions.

Visualization

Each of the mudras or hand positions and movements are best if visualized in a particular color. However, since each of the seven mudra groups of any particular series may change color as one proceeds, we've found it best to use the color of the first grandparent throughout the ritual movement rather than changing the color from movement to movement, however, you are free to do what feels best to you. Note that while there are eight basic mudra hand positions, each oracle will produce seven movement groups that are a combination of any of these eight mudras.

Chapter One:
The Golden Dragon

x
x
x
x
x
x
x

The Golden Dragon symbolizes creative action. If you are an artist of any sort, this is a great sign to get. If you are about to initiate any project, including business projects, or you are asking about starting something new this is a sign that says definitely proceed. It is strong and untiring and promises success to those who follow through with their intentions to completion.

If your question is spiritual in nature, it indicates that what you are doing or about to do is supported by the weight of the Universe. You are in the right place at the right time and now all you have to do is be sure that what you are doing is right or fair for everyone concerned and is in keeping with the laws of Nature, the Universe and the fairness that is part and parcel of Elfin being and of being in Elfin.

If your question has to do with obstacles you are facing, then the response would indicate that you need to get in touch with the Universe, align yours'elf with what is fair and right, and strive to become in harmony with the situation. Then success will come to you from the Divine Magic and nothing will be able to stop it.

The Golden Dragon also symbolizes a blessing upon you. In getting it, it means magic is heading your way. The Universe, the Shining Ones and the Divine Magic have heard your call and are responding at this very moment, sending you energy that you can use to resolve your current situation, create something greater and take a further step on the path to magical initiation, mastery and adeptship.

Mantra:

Tas Soch

Pronounced: tace sow-ch (rhymes with roach)

Meaning: Go Forth

Mudra:

Use mudra one for both dominant and assisting hands. Hold the assisting hand straight out from your shoulder with the palm downward. Hold the dominant hand with elbow bent, palm inward and outstretched fingers pointed upward as though you are holding a pistol in an old fashioned duel. Quickly arc the dominant hand downward, elbow now bent at an approximate 45° angle and pointing forward visualizing the colored light created by the movement of the arc.

Visualization:

Bright golden light.

Chapter Two: The White Unicorn

o
o
o
o
o
o
o

The White Unicorn is a symbol of purity but also of inspiration. It is supportive but not directive. It is also an indication that everything will unfold as it should in a step by step fashion and that all one needs to do is all that is required and necessary to complete the task or vision before one, doing each thing as time and circumstance demand. It requires nothing more of one than what one is capable of doing.

However, it also indicates that if you are in an assistant position that you do all you can to help the project succeed. Your job here is not to direct but to fulfill the directions as given. In this way, by fulfilling your purpose in this situation luck comes to you. The energy of this oracle is not one of the architect but of the builder who carries out the directions of the architect, following and executing hir (his/her) plans. It is not the aspect and energy of the teacher who guides the student by setting tasks before hir, but of the student who does hir best to complete the tasks given in order to learn all that sHe (she/he) can and master the skills that sHe seeks to learn.

Persistence and endurance are called for here. Patience and steadfastness are advised. This is not an energy of waiting but rather of slow but sure progress. If there are obstacles, set about removing them one at a time. Everything is a movement toward completion. Every step, even those that seem backwards, brings one closer (in time) to completion.

This is not a good sign for beginning something but for seeing things through, for completing things that are already in motion. Once one has done that one can move on to the new. It is a sign of good fortune but it is luck that comes after one has done all that one can and it usually arrives unexpectedly.

Mantra:

Ver wyl rakirtu

Pronounced: Veer will ray-kir (rhymes with fire) - two

Meaning: In all sincerity

Mudra:

Using mudra eight for both hands, place the assisting hand against one's waist at one's back with the palm facing outward and away from the body. Place the dominant hand with outstretched fingers pointing toward the opposite shoulder, palm toward one's body. Slowly, stretch out one's hand turning it over as one does so, so that the palm is upward and out from the body as though one's is offering something.

Visualization:

Bright Silver Light

Chapter Three: Sea Serpent

o
o
o
o
o
o
x

This oracle indicates the movement of the deep unconscious. You may sense that something is coming, something impending and this may very well make you feel uneasy. Receiving the Sea Serpent means that things are in motion on the unseen planes and it is best if you wait patiently and take no action until you are certain of what is going on. You may wish to prepare for various contingencies but to also "expect the unexpected," which is to say realize that no matter how much you prepare, things may turn out differently than you assumed that they might.

But you should not necessarily presume that things will go wrong. The admonition to hope for the best, while preparing for the worst, is apropos here, but you may also wish to prepare for the best and everything in between as well. Meditative silence and stillness of mind are recommended. Be like a cat with its tail flicking side to side as it prepares to pounce but bide your time and wait for the right moment or everything will be lost.

This is like a game in which it is not your turn and you can only consider what you may do if your opponent moves this way or that way. And even then, this is a game where there are more possible moves than anyone can foretell.

Mantra:

Verva tae dorwynli

Pronounced: Veer-vah tay door-win-lie

Meaning: Into the depths

Mudra:

Place both hands in mudra eight. Put the dominant hand over your heart. Have the assisting hand straight out in front of you, palm outward as though you are signaling someone to stop. Now, change the position of the hands so the dominant hand is outward in the stop position and the assisting hand is over your heart.

Visualization:

Bright white light

Chapter Four: The Red Dragon

x
x
x
x
x
x
o

The Red Dragon is a symbol of great power held temporarily in check. Everything is ready and waiting and one is mostly likely anxious to act, but the time has still not come and one must, if good fortune is to attend one's acts, await the right moment.

If you attempt to use force to achieve what you desire you will probably succeed, but there will be consequences and there will be pushback and this will only create more complications for you. As the saying goes, hold your horses. Having such great power, you no longer need to use force. Wait and all things will come to you. Then your actions will proceed naturally through time and circumstances and everything will turn out as you wish and good fortune will be the result.

This is a positive sign for any question if one has mastered the magical power of patience. You are on the verge of something great. Like a talented and beloved actor standing off stage awaiting hir (his/her) cue to go on, you just need to await the right moment to enter.

Mantra:

Ena ralt dart

Pronounced: E-nah rail-t dare-t

Meaning: With great force

Mudra:

With both hands in the mudra one position, place the assisting hand behind your back at the waist with palm outward. Have the dominant hand with outstretched fingers pointing toward the opposite shoulder. Bring the dominant hand forward and downward across the body so that the fingers end up with palm upward pointing to a place about five or six feet (about a meter and a half to two meters) in front of you.

Visualization:

Bright Yellow Light

Chapter Five: The Mother

o
x
o
o
o
x
x

The Mother is a sign of nurturing. It is giving by nature and other oriented. Thus getting this oracle indicates that one should invest one's energy into others. It is time to give gifts, to feed those you love, to nurture those you feel are worthy and who will use what you give them well.

This is also a symbol of giving birth and the struggles that entails. Help those who are struggling to give birth to their own s'elves, to creative projects toward creating a better life. Help ease your own projects into being, but realize that this is often a matter of awaiting the right moment then pushing for all one is worth. One must be patient until Nature signals the time and then one must put all one's energy toward the fulfillment of one's goals.

Thus, this is also an indication of new birth and all the flurry of activity that attends it. This will surely be exhausting but the rewards will be well worth it. You can relax later and recuperate, now that the time is upon you, you must act with the full power of your intent to bring things to fruition.

Mantra:

Hel darl an tae altu

Pronounced: Heal dare-l ane (rhymes with pain) tay ale-two

Meaning: Nurture well from the start

Mudra:

Have the dominant hand in mudra two and the assisting hand in mudra six. Have your assisting hand bent at the elbow and the hand at a forty-five degree angle to your shoulder, palm toward that shoulder. Have the dominant hand down by your side, palm inward toward your side and raise it up swiftly and directly forward from the body with a sudden twist, palm upward, arm outstretched and push it outward as it reaches its final point.

Visualization:

Radiant Violet light

Chapter Six: The Father

o
x
o
o
o
x
o

If you receive the Father this is an indication that one must persevere despite any difficulties. Often, at this point, one must take ones'elf in hand, so to speak, and be a bit hard on ones'elf, to carry on when one feels like giving up and urging others to do the same.

In that way, one determines ones'elf to set an example of strength and endurance, as well as fostering and encouraging those who are under one's direction or assisting one. One is at the beginning but needs to keep going otherwise everything may collapse. In military terms, one is establishing a beachhead. Therefore, this is a sign of good fortune if one endures. The whole effort is toward creating and establishing a successful beginning.

But let us remember that in giving birth, the father is, primarily, in an assisting role. His job for the most part is to support and encourage. It is still the mother who will do most of the work of giving birth and suffers nearly all the pain. A certain amount of compassion and empathy may therefore be advised. Do not push so much as nurture and inspire, help focus and encourage those who are doing most of the work. The pushing will be done mostly by others.

Mantra:

Tat El ba

Pronounced: Tate Eel bah

Meaning: As I do

Mudra:

Have the assisting hand in mudra six and the dominant hand in mudra two. Place the assisting hand behind one's back, palm outward, with hand up toward the shoulder blade of opposite shoulder. Place dominant hand toward opposite ear, palm inward toward the ear. Bring dominant hand swiftly forward and out from the shoulder, palm downward, outstretched fingers toward front.

Visualization:

Bright red light outlined by light blue light

Chapter Seven: The Fool

x
o
o
o
x
o
x

Getting the Fool can indicate that one is dealing with foolish individuals or those who are attempting or will attempt to deceive one, although usually this deception is not so much intentional but rather a result of the fact that this individual is actively and unknowingly, unconsciously or sometimes willfully deceiving hir (his/her) own self. This is not the action of the demonic but of the idiotic.

Thus in receiving this oracle one is cautioned to examine the facts carefully. To be certain that all that one is hearing is the truth and to remember that mere enthusiasm, while powerful and interesting, is not in itself an indication that an individual knows what they are talking about. Facts are almost never changed by wishful thinking or excited optimism.

Consider also that, if the individual you are dealing with is at least open minded, even while foolish, that you may be able to guide and educate hir. Alas, if the individual lacks this basic openness and willingness to learn, the situation is for the most part hopeless and it is better for all concerned if you simply ignore such individuals.

Mantra:

Teke el tae yer

Pronounced: Tea-key eel tay year

Meaning: Show me the way

Mudra:

Have dominant hand in mudra six and assisting hand in mudra seven. Mudra six is the hand of the bull or goat or horned god so popular in heavy metal, and mudra seven is a fist. Have the assisting hand with arm out, elbow bent, so the lower arm is at a right angle and parallel to the chest, palm downward. The dominant hand is also palm downward and outstretched so the wrist of the dominant hand crosses and is on top of the assisting hand. Now, jut both hands forward and away from the body about six inches forward of original position.

Visualization:

Brilliant blue light outlined in amber light

Chapter Eight: The Child

x
o
o
o
x
o
o

Receiving the Child indicates that one may be inexperienced in the issues that one is asking about or that one is dealing with those who are inexperienced and who need some mentoring. If it is you who is a novice concerning the question you have inquired about, then seek someone that you can trust who knows what they are doing, and who will guide you toward the right actions and directions.

If you are very experienced then there is probably someone else in this situation who is less than clear about what they are doing, although they may not admit that this is the case and in fact, may pretend otherwise. A certain amount of goodwill and tolerance is recommended here. Try to remember what it was like when you were first starting out, when you were in a similar situation.

Remember also that such inexperienced individuals tend to be fickle. They begin things with tremendous energy and enthusiasm and often quite a bit of boasting, but as soon as things get tough they abandon the project quickly, leaving you to bear the burden and the responsibility. You may not be able to count on them and you should know this from the start.

Mantra:

Ena thothådur

Pronounced: E-nah throw – thah – dure (as in endure)

Meaning: With expectation

Mudra:

Dominant hand should use mudra six and assisting hand mudra seven. Have both hands down by your sides palms inward toward body. Bring the dominant hand upward twisting it as you do, so that the elbow is bent, the outstretched fingers pointed to the ceiling or sky and the palm toward one's back.

Visualization:

Radiant blue light outlined by golden amber

Chapter Nine: The Panther

o
x
o
x
x
x
x

The Panther is a powerful response to any question. It does indicate that one should delay until the moment is right, but it also indicates tremendous power for action when that time arrives. This also often indicates that one has unseen powers, mystical powers that are hidden or that have not as yet manifested. Something comes. Something big is in motion and one need only be able to wait. The Divine Magic, the power of the Universe, favors you and will assist you. You need not worry that you won't achieve your goal. That is nearly certain. It is merely a matter of time. Relax. Everything is in motion. You have done your part and now you need only abide in patience awaiting your moment to act. When it comes you will be able to act with speed, power and force.

You may be feeling the powerful impending nature of what is to come and like a thunderstorm on the horizon, you may be uncertain about what will happen. But again, be at ease. The secret forces of the Universe are working on your behalf. Let them do their part. When you need to act it will be clear that the time has come because there will no longer be any doubt about it. If you are questioning if it is the right time or not, it isn't.

This oracle calls for strength. Only the strong are able to wait, the weak cannot help but rush forward and interfere before the time is right/ripe and in doing so interfere with the cosmic forces that seek to help them. And one must deal with what is real. Unrealistic expectations and illogical hopes will not lead you to success. Look at the situation as it really is and the spirits will guide you toward what you wish it to be.

Mantra:

Våherdas tae onst

Pronounced: Vah – here – dace tay ohnst (sounds like cone with an st)

Meaning: Awaiting the moment

Mudra:

Put the dominant hand in mudra one and the assisting hand in mudra six. Have the assisting hand across one's waist at the front, palm inward to body and the dominant hand over the assisting hand connected at the wrist so the outstretched fingers are uppermost. Loop the dominant hand forward, under, around and back up, keeping the wrists connected, until the hands are back in their original position.

Visualization:

Yellow light outlined by bright blue

Chapter Ten: The Banshee

o
x
o
x
x
x
o

Traditionally the Banshee, or Bean Sidhe (fairy woman) proclaims that someone in one's family (usually of fairy blood) is about to die. Drawing this oracle signifies that you are being warned. There is something dangerous ahead of you on the path and you need to proceed with great caution and care. You need not fear, for fear will do you no good at all. And the potential danger is just that, potential, and not necessarily fated or destined to be. If you act with care you can encounter it and go beyond it without harm coming to you or failure attending your efforts. But you must pay attention to the small things as well as the large and do your very best in all that you do.

Don't feel that things will inevitably go wrong. This is just a bend in the road and while it is a narrow turn on a steep precipice, it is one that you can navigate successfully if you are heedful and cognizant of its dangers. The advice here is to keep going, perhaps slowly for a time until the way is less dangerous, but continue moving forward until the danger passes.

It is important to hold in mind that even though you are moving very slowly, you are still making progress and really that is what is important. That and keeping the progress going no matter how slow it may be.

Mantra:

El polth tae mes

Pronounced: Eel pole-th tay miece (rhymes with niece)

Meaning: I heed the signs

Mudra:

Let the dominant hand assume position number one and the assisting hand position number two. Have the assisting hand behind your back, palm outward, knuckles against one's buttocks. Have the dominant hand by one's side pointing downward, palm toward one's leg, and bring it slowly up so the elbow is bent and the outstretched fingers are pointing toward the ceiling/sky and then snap the hand quickly forward and back as though cracking a whip.

Visualization:

Bright green light

Chapter Elven: The Orc

x

x

x

o

x

o

x

If you receive this oracle then it means that someone or ones are deliberately obstructing you or intend to do so. This is direct opposition and obstruction and is likely to lead to conflict. One is cautioned about engaging in this conflict without being certain that one is in the right, but even then, conflict is likely to be costly and time consuming to all the parties involved. Diplomacy is advised if it is at all possible. Certainly, the action of attempting to reach compromise and agreement will be in your favor if the situation does evolve, or devolve really, into conflict. This is especially true if, in the course of time, the conflict leads to an arbiter or judge making a final settlement in the matter.

It would be wise at this point, before continuing, to pause and examine the situation carefully. Also, using the adage to know your enemy as you know yours'elf or know your enemy like the back of your hand, to know what you opponent actually wants and intends and to see if you can yield in any way without giving up what is essential to your own needs and goals is important to remember. It is quite possible that a compromise may be reached by giving way on things that are not really vital to you.

Know this, however, if the situation does lead to conflict you may lose and even if you win this individual will most likely find other ways to obstruct you in the future. Thus, again, it is best if a mutually satisfying compromise can be reached.

Mantra:

Pa kon jän

Pronounced: Pah cone jan

Meaning: Tread not here

Mudra:

Have the dominant hand in mudra position six and the assisting hand in number one. Have the assisting hand with fingers pointed downward arm down and against one's body, palm forward. The dominant should be across the body, palm toward body with the index and little finger resting on either side of the inner elbow. Move both hands so that they cross to the other side of the body. The dominant hand flips over so it is now palm upward, arm to the body bent at a ninety-degree angle so the hand is pointing forward. The assisting hand also flips and crosses over, palm downward, and the outstretched fingers land upon the upturned wrist of the other hand as though you are taking your own pulse.

Visualization:

Golden blue light

Chapter Twelve: The Goblin

x
x
x
o
x
o
o

In receiving The Goblin one is put on notice that there is someone who is working behind the scenes against you. It is unlikely that they will do so directly. Which is to say they are unlikely to confront you or oppose you to your face. Instead, they will work in the shadows endeavoring to block and undo whatever it is that you wish to achieve. It is quite possible that this individual is even pretending to be your friend, or at least, friendly on the surface.

This person is well aware that what sHe (she/he) is doing is wrong, which is why the individual isn't opposing you directly. If sHe felt justified in doing what sHe's doing, sHe would declare hir (his/her) righteousness in doing so. However, since sHe is certain that what sHe is doing would not meet social approval, and is probably afraid of your reaction if you knew what sHe was up to, sHe works in secret.

Thus, in receiving this oracle you should be extra careful and examine all that is going on. You may discover what is happening. You may even, if you follow the influences back to their source, discover who is doing it, but even if you confront hir, sHe is unlikely to admit it and will surely continue behind your back. However, knowing the truth can be helpful and knowing that one must be particularly cautious in one's dealings is very important as well.

Mantra:

Hed alsåon yer

Pronounced: Heed ale – sah – ohn (rhymes with phone) year

Meaning: Seek another way

Mudra:

Have your dominant hand in mudra six and the assisting hand assume mudra one. Place the assisting hand with palm toward body, elbow bent, with the hand resting against one's collar bone and the outstretched fingers bent over and resting upon one's shoulder. Have the outstretched fingers of the dominant hand resting on the lower arm of the assisting hand, just above the elbow, palm toward one's body. Bring the dominant hand upward to one's forehead, palm still toward one, so that it appears rather like those who put horns behind your head when you are taking a picture without you knowing it, only in the front. Then flick that hand quickly forward and back so that the hand ends to the front of and the right side of one's face.

Visualization:

Brilliant blue light outlined in gold

Chapter Thirteen: The Warrior

o
o
o
o
x
o
x

In receiving this oracle, you are directed to take action as soon as you are prepared and ready to do so. Be sure your ducks are in a row, as the saying goes, but as soon as they are, get moving. There is no time to waste and there is much that can be achieved if you act with confidence and certainty and act as soon as possible. Put aside your doubts and uncertainties and get going.

And remember, if you need help, ask for it. You may need allies in this and if you have fostered your friends, your kindred and the friendly spirits there will be those that you can call upon to aid you in your work. The important thing is to make progress now when the time is right. Do not delay, except to get organized. If you have prepared before hand, and have been waiting, then the time is now. Be strong, be courageous, take action, success is assured.

However, it is quite possible that the action you need take will be that of the director of the action. Those you call to aid you will need your guidance as to what needs to be done and how to do it. Be like a commander at the center of his army. Inspire your helpers and make clear the goals that need to be achieved and the reasons for achieving them. If you can do this effectively then all should go well and great success is yours. Now is the time to lead.

Mantra:

La jolv stran

Pronounced: Lah joel-v strain

Meaning: By might direct

Mudra:

Assume position six with your dominant hand and position eight with your assisting hand. Place the assisting hand in front of your breastbone with palm upward. Put the dominant hand, palm down, into the palm of the assisting hand, resting upon it, with the outstretched fingers pointing away from the body.

Slowly but surely and with determination, keeping the hands in contact, move both hands forward and away from your body.

Visualization:

Luminous blue light outlined in silver

Chapter Fourteen: The Sage

o
o
o
o
x
o
o

The Sage indicates that you may be wise to consult those who know more than you and have greater experience concerning the issues you have asked about. If you have received this as one of the grandparents then it is best to seek this advice early in your efforts to achieve what you desire. If you receive it as one of the parents, then it is likely that someone will offer you advice in the process of this fulfillment and even if you don't agree with the advice, listen carefully and give it due consideration. There just may be an element within it that will be valuable to you. And if you receive this as the child (see introduction) then it is likely that what you will gain from this experience in wisdom and in a greater understanding of how to proceed from thenceforth or in the future if you should seek to accomplish the same thing again. You will be able thus to do it even better the second or third time around.

It is also possible that in receiving this oracle, particularly if you receive it in the last place, the place of the child, that others may look up to you and come to you for advice and you are advised therefore to consider their needs and desires seriously and to do the best that you can for them. To give their situation thorough consideration and not simply say a few convenient homilies or adages in order to fob them off. Consider how you would like to be treated if you were in their position. And remember, those who come to you for help now may very well be in a position to aid you at some future date. You are not only giving advice; not merely sharing your experiential wisdom; you are creating potential alliances for the future. Do this and all will turn out well.

Mantra:

Joul turyl sojïn

Pronounced: Jo – yule two – rill sow-j - in

Meaning: Through insight gained

Mudra:

Have the dominant hand in mudra six and the assisting hand in mudra eight. Place the assisting hand on one's same side hip, palm to body, and position the dominant hand, palm down across the body at the level of the breastbone. Move the dominant hand downward in a loop and then upward and out from the body, around and then down again in one continuous circle, coming to rest with outstretched fingers pointing to the floor/ground, palm pointed behind one.

Visualization:

Bright blue light outlined in white

Chapter Fifteen: The Leprechauns

o
x
o
o
o
o
x

On receiving this oracle, one is advised to save part of what one has, or one's energy, for later. Don't do everything at once. Don't expend all your energy in one go. Or as the old folks used to tell us when they gave us money, don't spend it all in one place. This oracle calls us to remember that the process of success in terms of the question asked will take some time and is an incremental unfolding of events. It doesn't matter how much energy you put into things or how strong you are or how powerful, you just can't force it to completion before the time is right. So save your energy, or some of it at least, for later. This is a matter that will take perseverance.

This oracle also informs us that this is an unfolding situation and that there is more that has yet to happen that will influence what is occurring. The outcome is not yet determined and it is good under such circumstances to proceed toward success but realize that it is also wise, in this instance, to wait awhile and then inquire about the situation once again. It is quite possible that in a relatively short time the outlook will have altered and the way things seem now may not be how things eventually turn out.

Yet, even though that is the case, it is best to proceed as though success is probable, even likely. The outcome may still be in doubt, but you should not be. Keep the goal in mind and continue on slowly but steadily. Repairing and correcting anything that may go wrong as you continue and then, when you feel the time is right, throw the oracle again and see what it says.

Mantra:

La rimta lun

Pronounced: Lah rhyme-tah loon

Meaning: By hidden light

Mudra:

Have dominant hand in position eight and assisting hand in position six. Have the assisting hand in front of the body, just under the belly button, palm toward the body. Place the dominant hand over the assisting hand, palm inward, covering the outstretched fingers of the assisting hand. Move both hands so the dominant hand comes up, fingers pointed toward the ceiling/sky, elbow bent, palm pointed behind one. Simultaneously, bring the assisting hand up so the outstretched fingers land on either side of the lower wrist of the dominant hand, beneath the little finger along the narrow ridge of the hand.

Visualization:

Bright white light outlined by blue

Chapter Sixteen: The Brownies

o
x
o
o
o
o
o

On receiving the Brownies, one is encouraged to pitch in and lend a helping hand. If you can't work on the big things, then do whatever you can. Take care of the details, however small, for by dealing with them now you will be saving yours'elf time and potential trouble later on.

Also, this oracle advises one to hold on, hold steady and don't give up. Be steadfast. No matter how things may look at present, continue on your course, things will work out eventually. It is true that things may have slowed down to a snail's pace, but don't let that concern you. There are ebbs and flows in every situation and life, and in the course of time, things will pick up and begin moving again. Don't let little progress convince you that there is no progress. And even if there has been no progress, that doesn't mean that things won't progress later on. If this is what you truly desire then hold on and do whatever it is you can, no matter how minute and seemingly insignificant to move things along.

It is also quite possible that others are depending upon you. That they are looking toward you for guidance and inspiration. If you give up, they will likely do so as well. Consider well how your actions will affect others. What is your responsibility in this situation?

Mantra:

La murtenïn tålli

Pronounced: La muir – teen – in tahl – lie

Meaning: By unseen paths

Mudra:

Dominant hand should be in mudra eight and assisting hand in mudra six. Place the assisting hand behind your back, palm away from the body, so that the outstretched fingers can be seen peeking out from the front. Have the dominant hand over your heart, palm on body, and swing it down in an arc to your side, so the fingers are pointing to the floor/ground and the palm is toward the rear.

Visualization:

Glowing silver light outlined by blue

Chapter Seventeen: The Pooka

x
x
o
x
x
x
x

In drawing this oracle, one may assume that things are not as they seem and is cautioned to look more closely at what is going on, as well as more carefully at those one is involved with in this matter. It is also possible that someone who seems entirely in favor of this project will change hir (his/her) mind and be against it or abandon it later, or just the opposite that someone who is not in favor of it will be swayed in time toward its fulfillment.

It is also possible that someone is seeking to take you for a ride and the outcome may not be entirely pleasant for you. Again, proceed with caution and don't hurry into anything. Check everything out before you continue further. Of course, it is also possible that you may seem to have no choice in the matter, that you have been drawn into things by those who are more powerful and have more influence than you, or those whose approval it is that you seek. However, remember, they won't respect you for having let yours'elf be used or fooled.

At the same time, it is perhaps advisable for you to pretend to be fooled without being so. To let others think that they are deceiving you while keeping the truth within your own heart and being ready to withdraw when you need to do so. In that way, just when they thought they had you in their net you will slip away from them. In any case, stay alert but appear a bit oblivious.

Mantra:

Ver nalf tasemïn

Pronounced: Veer nail-f tay – seem - in

Meaning: In shape disguised

Mudra:

Place dominant hand in mudra one position and assisting hand in mudra five. Have the arms crossed at the chest, dominant wrist over the wrist of the assisting hand, each hand pointing to the opposite shoulder, palms to the body. Bring the dominant hand forward and out so the arm is extended, the hand palm downward but bent slightly upward at a forty-five degree angle from the wrist.

Visualization:

Brilliant yellow green

Chapter Eighteen: The Kelpie

x
x
o
x
x
x
o

In receiving the Kelpie it is likely that someone is manipulating your feelings or will attempt to do so concerning the issue in question. This effort is most likely due to the fact that they wish to cloud your mind with your emotions so you will not be able think clearly about what is going on, or to redirect your mind toward those things that are actually irrelevant to the situation. They seek to overwhelm you with trivia.

It is also possible that this is quite innocent in its way. That the individual is not so much attempting to interfere with what you are doing but to simply draw attention to their own selves and their interests and problems, rather like little children, totally absorbed in their own selves and oblivious to anyone else's needs or energy. In such a case, a certain firm but considerate response is called for. Let them know that at this time, you simply must concentrate upon what you are doing and will have time for them and their interests later.

At the same time, it is also possible that you are the one who is called upon to restrain a more powerful person or force and you don't have the energy or authority to do so directly and so you must use small delaying or restraining tactics to keep them from proceeding down a course that will do no one any good in the long run, even themselves, although they are unlikely to listen to reason, thus subtlety is called for. The disinterested truth without emotion or personal involvement sometimes does the trick.

Mantra:

Sofdas faron

Pronounced: Sof (rhymes with oaf) – dace fay - rone

Meaning: Slipping away

Mudra:

Let the dominant hand assume the first mudra and the assisting hand assume the fifth position. Have the elbow bent and the dominant arm and hand upward with the outstretched fingers pointing toward the ceiling and the palm toward the back. Have the fingers of the assisting hand just above the inner elbow of the dominant arm cradled by the bent arm. Bring the dominant hand forward twisting it so that the fingers point straight ahead like you are shooting a gun while the assisting hand simultaneously slides forward along the arm and settles at the wrist of the dominant hand.

Visualization:

Bright yellow outlined in radiant green

Chapter Nineteen: The Pixies

x
x
x
o
x
x
x

You may just have to be a bit tricky at this point in your progress. You may be called to lead people away from what is unimportant to what is really vital even though they don't seem to realize this is so. This may be rather like capturing a child's attention from what sHe shouldn't be playing with in order to protect hir.

In receiving this oracle, you are called to perform a little social sleight of hand, to direct the individuals involved elsewhere with a bit of distraction or magical misdirection. It is quite possible that these individuals are more powerful than you. Thus speaking truth to power in this case calls for a bit of sly maneuvering. It you can do this well, if you can tease them without making them angry, you may just get away with it and accomplish the task set before you, which is to drop subtle hints about what should or should not be.

This may be achieved if you suggest to the individuals involved potential difficulties that may arise in a concerned way and for their benefit. They may not wish to hear these things, but they cannot deny the truth of them, or should not for their own good, and cannot accuse you of interference when you are clearly concerned for their own wellbeing. If you can make all this as friendly as possible, all will go well.

Mantra:

Erst sakla båïn

Pronounced: Ear-st (rhymes with pierced) sake – lah bah – in

Meaning: Most cleverly done

Mudra:

Place the dominant hand in mudra four and the assisting hand in mudra one. Have the dominant hand over the assisting hand, crossed at the wrists about stomach level. Move both hands together in a loop, down, inward and up to the original position and then jut both hands forward so the outstretched fingers are pointing to the front.

Visualization:

Luminous purple outlined by bright yellow

Chapter Twenty: The Imp

x
x
x
o
x
x
o

Here you are dealing with someone who is interfering with what you desire, for no better reason than to control things and manipulate you. Such individuals' only interest is in creating a bit of chaos. We could call this the Joker factor. They delight in destruction and just want to see it all fall down so they can watch the confusion and conflict ensue.

Alas, this interference may not be direct or obvious. You may have to follow the problems back to their source, but even if you discover who is behind things, it is unwise to confront them directly and unlikely to do any good if you do. Simply continue on, doing your best, and being aware that there is someone out there who is working against you.

It would be nice if there was a solution to this problem, but really there is little you can do but forge onward and trust that in time this individual will find other things to capture hir interest, for such beings are never satisfied with anything and are always seeking to interfere. So, this isn't personal, or it is unlikely to be. It is just a sort of demented hobby from a person who, deep within hirself, is a miserable human being.

Mantra:

Enåkon nalorcara

Pronounced: E – nah – cone nay – lore – care – rah

Meaning: Without interference

Mudra:

Assume position four for the dominant hand and mudra one for the assisting hand. Place the assisting hand so the palm is toward the body and the outstretched fingers touching the opposite shoulder. Have the dominant hand, elbow bent, palm toward the front, outstretched fingers toward the ceiling/sky. Bring the dominant hand down to one's side, palm now toward rear, and then bring it up to the opposite shoulder so it is over the assisting arm with wrists crossed.

Visualization:

Radiant violet outlined by bright yellow

Chapter Twenty-One: The Sidhe

o
o
o
x
x
x
x

In receiving this oracle, one has fallen under the light and guidance of the Sidhe and will be experiencing a certain degree of luck and blessing in one's life. This luck will mostly likely come from an unexpected source or in a surprising way, and one may at first be a bit uncertain or doubtful about its meaning, but in time it will become clear that this is a good thing for you and is definitely a good sign in terms of the question asked, particularly if you receive this in the first or last place, the first grandparent or the child.

You may be at peace, at least for a bit, for things are going your way and you need only follow through with what you already have going. Or if you are asking about starting something new then, yes, the way is open to you and you are free, even encouraged, to initiate action. There are higher forces at work who wish to help you succeed and will do what they can upon the invisible planes to make that so.

You must have done something right because the great powers of Elfin are smiling on you and you should keep up the good work. Understand, this is a blessing upon you. A reward that you have earned and you may feel satisfied in the knowledge that this is the case.

Mantra:

U marynli sushoïn

Pronounced: You may – ren – lie sue – show – in

Meaning: Of secrets whispered

Mudra:

Put the dominant hand in mudra one and the assisting hand in mudra eight. Have both hands, palms toward each other, at the forehead with lower knuckle of the thumbs against one's third eye. Move both hands outward to one's sides as far as one's arms will reach, like Jesus on the cross, and then bring the hands and palms together again at one's breastbone.

Visualization:

Golden light outlined by silver

Chapter Twenty-Two: The Seelie

o
o
o
x
x
x
o

In receiving this oracle, you may feel blessed, however, it is very important that you do what is right and fair for everyone involved in the situation. If you try to do things that are not in keeping with fairness then eventually things will turn out very badly for you concerning this question. If you have in some way cut corners that you shouldn't have or have been less than fair to some involved, now is the time to set things straight and repair whatever damage has occurred or prevent any from occurring if it is not too late to do so.

Remember, this is not punishment for you. This is not bad karma coming to roost. It is really a blessing in the form of a warning to stay upon the path and do what is right for everyone. If you do that then rewards will surely come your way and all that you hoped to achieve will come to fruition.

It is true that the higher powers, the Shining Ones, are observing you and you may feel that strange feeling you get when someone is watching you but you don't know where they are or sensation you get when your teachers are standing over you as you are taking a test. But, remember that the reason they are checking you out is because you have attracted their attention and they have seen potential in you. Now you just need to do your best.

Mantra:

La lun maryoldas

Pronounced: Lah loon mare – yole - dace

Meaning: By light unfolding

Mudra:

With the dominant hand in mudra one and the assisting hand in mudra eight, palms downward, assisting hand over dominant hand at chest level, rotate the dominant hand around so the outstretched fingers are pointing upward toward the sky/ceiling, palm toward opposite side of body and the fingers of the assisting hand, still in same position, are now touching the inner wrist of the dominant hand.

Visualization:

Yellow light outlined by white light

Chapter Twenty-Three: The Grimlens

x

x

x

o

o

o

x

Unfortunately, if you receive this oracle then it is likely that the answer to your question is no, or not now, or not enough energy for it. This is especially true if this is found in the first place, which is the first grandparent, or the last place, the position of the child, which is the outcome. If you get it at the first place it may indicate that everything will be bogged down from the get go and be near impossible to get started at all. In the last place, it may indicate that after all your hard work and investment of time and energy that things will fall apart and simply not turn out the way you wanted them to. Anywhere in between and it is an indication that at some point in the process things will become stagnant, but it is possible that you can get them going again. Where you receive it in the reading will determine how close to the beginning or the end of the project that this is likely to occur.

If you are not determined to pursue this thing then it might be wiser to give up now and not waste any more of your time and energy on it. However, if this is something that you feel you absolutely must have or desire to do then realize that in pursuing this path that it is unlikely to be easy and perseverance is sure to be called for. At any rate, the time is not quite right, but that doesn't mean that later on the situation won't change. You may have to be strict with yours'elf. You may have to budget yours'elf and you may have to lower your expectations. The realization may be far less perfect than you envisioned. But if you are sure this is what you want then proceed; just don't expect it to be easy.

Mantra:

Ver tae dasårli

Pronounced: Veer tay day – sahr (rhymes with far) - lie

Meaning: In the shadows

Mudra:

Take position eight for the dominant hand and position one for the assisting hand. Have the assisting hand elbow to side, lower arm and hand forward, at a forty-five degree angle to the body, outstretched fingers uppermost. Have the dominant hand by one's same side cheek, also, fingers toward ceiling/sky, also at about forty-five degree angle to face. Bring the dominant hand down upon the assisting hand, twice, in a chopping motion. On the second time let it rest on top of and across assisting hand and move both forward, away from the body, as the dominant hand turns palm downward and covers the top of the assisting hand.

Visualization:

Silver light outlined by golden light

Chapter Twenty-Four: The Red Caps

X
X
X
O
O
O
O

This is seldom a good sign. Here you have people who are vindictive and interfering because they believe they have a right to be so. Examine the situation and see if indeed there is any justification for their interference. If there is, try to come to some resolution and agreement with them, for this, at least, will enable you to proceed. If they can see that they will benefit from the situation, too, then they may just get out of your way.

Although, it could be that they are interfering because they have for some unjustified reason, mostly likely of a totally irrational nature and born of their own ignorance and prejudice, decided that they should do so. You could try to persuade them not to interfere, however, since they are irrational beings, logic is unlikely to be of any use to you and facts will have no power for they simply believe other things and the truth to their minds is whatever they believe it to be no matter what the facts are. In such a case there is little you can do but protect yours'elf as best you may and continue onward, in secret as much as possible, so they won't be able to see what you are doing, and thus cannot interfere further.

Still, this is not the best of situations, and there is no real solution to this problem beyond giving them absolutely no energy or attention so that they will eventually go elsewhere and bother someone else. We elves, however, wish you the best of luck with this.

Mantra:

Ena ti arota

Pronounced: E – nah tie a – row – tah

Meaning: With due caution

Mudra:

Assume mudra eight for the dominant hand and mudra one for the assisting hand. Have both hands at stomach height, dominant hand over assisting hand, palms toward body. Keeping the assisting hand in place, bring the dominant hand outward in an arc and at the last moment flick it like you are shooing a pest away.

Visualization:

White light outlined by yellow light

Chapter Twenty-Five: The Faeries

x
x
x
x
o
x
x

On receiving this oracle you can be certain that there are individuals and spirits that support you concerning this issue and will do what they can to aid and assist you as best they are able from whatever dimension they are upon. The Faeries are with you and you can feel truly blessed that this is so.

In as much as possible, seek the help and frasority (fraternity/sorority) /fellowship with your kindred for this is truly a situation where numbers count and we are stronger together than apart. Remember that sincerity and genuineness of feeling is all important here and material demonstrations of friendship are less so, but that being said it would not hurt to reward your friends and make it worth their while as much as you can do so. At the very least, let them know how very much you value their aid and support.

It may also be the case that you will be called upon to aid and support one of your friends. Remember that in doing so you not only show your caring for them but increase the possibility of positive interaction between you and them in the future and also increase the likelihood that they will come to your aid when needed. It never hurts to have them in your debt as long as you don't remind them of this fact.

Mantra:

Fef tat na bartis

Pronounced: Feef (rhymes with thief) tate nah bare - tice

Meaning: Light as a feather

Mudra:

Put the dominant hand in mudra three and the assisting hand in mudra one. Place the outstretched fingers of both hands in front of you so the first and second fingers of mudra one are against the third and ring finger of mudra three, forming a triangle to your body. Flip both hands upward and outward, so they come to rest on their respective sides pointing upward at a forty-five degree angle to the body.

Visualization:

Golden orange light

Chapter Twenty-Six: The Familiar

x
x
x
x
o
x
o

This is the oracle of the Familiar or trusted aid and assistant, rather like an executive secretary or a President's head of staff or chief advisor. This person can be trusted to take on a great deal of the work that you have in mind and thus this is a good sign to get as long as you treat this individual with respect and honor this individual for hir expertise. It would be very unwise to regard this person with disrespect or to make them feel less than or inferior. This is your primary and stalwart supporter. If it weren't for this individual, others would be unlikely to follow you or support you. Make this person know that even though they work for you and assist you that you respect hir as an equal. If you don't actually respect this individual then you have the wrong helper.

If you have such a person in your life then you are truly blessed. If you don't have such a being, then look around and see who might fill this bill. If you can't find someone on the physical plane then consider summoning some spirit that you can trust to aid and help you. Mutual and shared success is a keen motivation for nearly every spirit. So consider what is in it for the person assisting you and make it worth hir while to continue. Then, great success will be yours.

This is also a sign that you can leave this project in another's competent hands. You don't need to micromanage.

Mantra:

Ena yoc solana

Pronounced: E – nah yoke so – lay - nah

Meaning: With trust absolute

Mudra:

Have the dominant hand in mudra three and the assisting hand in mudra one. Place the outstretched fingers of the assisting hand so they are touching the middle of the palm of the dominant hand. Both hands at the level of the solar plexus, assisting hand palm downward, dominant hand outstretched fingers toward ceiling/sky. Leaving the assisting hand as is, move the dominant hand to its own side, elbow still bent but outward from the side and palm forward and fingers still toward ceiling/sky. Then, in one fluid motion, bring the dominant hand forward and downward to one's front, turning the palm so it's facing the opposite side, in a strong motion as though directing traffic.

Visualization:

Yellow orange light

Chapter Twenty-Seven: The Elves

x
o
x
x
x
x
x

Receiving this oracle is a boon. It is a sign of great luck and a blessing upon your life in regard to the question you have put to the oracle. This luck doesn't require anything of you except to continue on you way with sincerity doing your best for yours'elf and all your others. A certain amount of modesty and kindness, however, would not be amiss for those virtues draw blessings to all who truly display them. The powers of Elfin support you and their radiance will illuminate the way.

However, it is important to understand that their actions and effects are not forceful in nature, but will achieve the needed results through an application of grace and restraint. If you imitate their actions in the way in which you proceed then all you do will be favored by them, and you will be uplifted thereby.

Understand, this is not the action of pushing or pulling but of allowing. Confidence in what you are doing is highly advised. You may fake it, if you feel you need to do so, but really, it is unnecessary. You may be confident that the kindred have your back and desire your success as though it were their own. So relax and continue onward. Success at this juncture is assured. If you receive this oracle in the first or last place, it is considered particularly powerful.

Mantra:

Elsa murcyrnïn

Pronounced: Eel – sah muir – cern- in

Meaning: Joy unbounded

Mudra:

Dominant hand assumes mudra one and assisting hand takes up mudra three. Have the assisting hand, elbow bent, with outstretched fingers pointing to opposite shoulder. Have the dominant hand across body with outstretched fingers touching the elbow of the assisting hand. Both palms toward body. Leaving the assisting hand in place, bring the dominant hand up, elbow bent to its own side ear, palm toward ear, bottom of hand forward, as though you are flicking something over your shoulder.

Visualization:

Golden light outlined by orange light

Chapter Twenty-Eight: The Shining Ones

x
o
x
x
x
x
o

The Shining Ones are rather like angels, only beings that have been through what we are now experiencing and have evolved beyond. Thus they know what we are going through and have great compassion for us, even while they will do whatever is necessary to get us to where we need to go.

To get this oracle is a sign that higher powers have taken an interest in what you are doing. Whether this is a good thing or not greatly depends upon what you are up to and the integrity with which you are pursuing your goals. If what you desire benefits all concerned then you can be sure that things will turn out well for you and them. If you are only pursuing your own interests, this is not necessarily wrong unless it comes at the unwarranted expense of and harms others. Be sure what you are doing is in harmony with the forces of evolution and you can be certain of success.

Still, you can expect a certain amount of interference from the Shining Ones. As we say, this is surely to your benefit even if it doesn't immediate appear to be so. Eventually you will see that everything is turning out just the way it was always meant to.

Mantra:

Tabitreradase lotymvessa

Pronounced: Tay – by – tree – ray – dace low – tim – veece - sah

Meaning: Illuminating everything

Mudra:

Dominant hand assumes position one and assisting hand is in position three. Have the assisting hand at the breastbone, palm inward toward body. Place the dominant hand at your side outstretched fingers pointing to the floor/earth, palm toward body. Bring the dominant hand up, elbow bent, outstretched fingers touching forehead, palm toward face as though saluting.

Visualization:

Yellow light outlined by orange light

Chapter Twenty-Nine: The Dryad

o
o
o
x
o
o
x

The Dryad symbolizes being in harmony with Nature and thus also of being in harmony with one's social environment. If you are in harmony with your surroundings then this is surely a good sign for you. If you are out of harmony with your environment or the situation you find yours'elf within then do all that you can to reestablish that harmony.

This oracle advises to you fit in as best you may. This doesn't necessarily mean that you should change to be like everyone around you, but a certain amount of camouflage and quiet reticence and, indeed, a bit of modesty so you are not a rough edge in the social circle may be helpful. Get along with everyone as best you may and the situation will go smoothly.

Here success is to be achieved by greasing the wheels of social interaction and paying close attention to what others are saying and doing, and adapting to the best of your ability. Then things will turn out well and the movement toward success will be eased.

Mantra:

Arae tae aldali

Pronounced: Air – ray tay ale – dah - lie

Meaning: Among the trees

Mudra:

Have the dominant hand in mudra position seven and the assisting hand in mudra eight. Elbows bent have the assisting hand meeting the dominant hand at chest level, the dominant hand in the palm of the assisting hand. Move the dominant hand across the body so that it is pushing the assisting hand until the assisting hand is in line with and in front of its shoulder, fingers pointing up at a forty-five degree angle.

Visualization:

Radiant amber light outlined in silver

Chapter Thirty: The Owl

o
o
o
x
o
o
o

There are things going on in secret that you need to discover. This is not to say that there are conspiracies, but rather there are certain tricks and tips that can help you toward success. This is esoteric knowledge. Find someone who has already succeeded in reference to this issue and seek hir advice. This is an oracle of hidden doorways and secret passageways and other unseen means that will make everything easier once you know them. The idea that it is not what you know but who you know is germane here. Knowing the one who knows is the key to success in this situation.

The right method of approach is important, however. One must be aware of one's own lack of knowledge and one's dependence upon the other. A certain humility is called for and due deference to the individual one seeks as one's benefactor. Yet, obsequiousness is to be avoided. Maintaining one's personal dignity while acknowledging the superior knowledge of the other is advised.

And an introductory gift is ever wise. It is a sign of respect and an indication that you value the individual whose assistance you seek and know that hir time is valuable as well. Follow the hints that this individual offers and then all will go well.

Mantra:

Joul varud kenvu

Pronounced: Jo – yule vay – rude keen - view

Meaning: Through silent knowledge

Mudra:

The dominant hand should be in mudra seven, which is a fist, and the assisting hand in mudra eight. Have the assisting hand covering and in front of the dominant hand at stomach level, then bring the assisting hand upward and back down again as though giving anyone looking from the front a quick peek at the dominant hand.

Visualization:

Bright amber light outlined in white

Chapter Thirty-One: The Nymph

o
o
x
o
o
o
x

This oracle suggests the power of joy in movement. Your enthusiasm will delight others and they will more eagerly assist you. Show your delight in this matter. Express your optimism openly and success will be yours. If you approach this issue with dread, you are unlikely to succeed. Don't be hesitant either. A new day is dawning and the sun is shining upon you and you may jump for joy and not have cause to regret it.

If others join in your optimistic mood that is all to the better. For then great things may be accomplished and truly, as we elven say, the more the merrier and the easier and lighter the load. It is in just this way that we may gain support for great undertakings and if we look to the future our visions may take on a shining aura of possibility.

It is in this fashion that we unite with the Divine Magic that is the source of all success and possibility. In this moment of ecstatic union with our kindred we unite with the Divine and can see that all things wondrous are possible. We rise above mundane concerns and perceive that the delight of our union will resonate through time long after every material accomplishment has passed away and been forgotten.

Mantra:

Farnfey matiïn

Pronounced: Fair-n – fay may – tie – in

Meaning: Pleasure shared

Mudra:

Position the dominant hand in mudra eight and the assisting hand in mudra two. Place your hands in front of you, fingers pointing forward, elbows bent at your sides, outstretched fingertips of the assisting hand touching the corresponding fingers on the dominant hand. Move the hands forward together and then part them, each going toward its own side as though you are parting the waves.

Visualization:

White light outlined by red

Chapter Thirty-Two: The Dwarves

o
o
x
o
o
o
o

What is called for now is industrious application of effort and a persistence and duration in doing so. But even more, one needs to approach this effort with a certain joy in doing it. It is this joy of movement toward one's goal that will lead one to success. Delighting in what you are doing, you make progress easily and the effort itself becomes rewarding. The Disney image of the dwarves in Snow White whistling while they work is a good example of this. It is important to enjoy your activity. It is a form of evocation intriguing the spirits with your efforts and enticing them to assist you.

If you have others that can join you in this endeavor, that is even better. If you sing together as you work, like the old image of bargemen singing as they poled the river, this will unite your efforts and make the job a lot easier. The key here is to make your activity toward this goal as easy and fun as possible so you look forward to doing it and do not dread the effort you must expend to accomplish what you wish.

It may actually require a bit of effort to learn to take delight in your work. But it will be well worth it. Then everything you do will be worth doing just in the doing of it and all will go well and success will be assured.

Mantra:

Ena murrolbådas ketrora

Pronounced: E – nah muir – roll – bah – dace key – trow - rah

Meaning: With unstinting perseverance

Mudra:

The dominant hand assumes position eight and the assisting hand takes up mudra two. Elbow bent at your sides, have your assisting hand forward and to the center of the body at a ninety degree angle to the arm and forty-five degree angle to the body, palm facing to the opposite side. Have the dominant hand over the assisting hand, palm down, so it is covering the thumb and hand but not the outstretched fingers. Then, keeping the assisting hand in place, move the dominant hand forward across the outstretched fingers of the assisting hand and out and forward from the body as though you are casting something away from you.

Visualization:

Silver light outlined by bright red

Chapter Thirty-Three: The Sylphs

o
x
x
o
o
x
x

The Sylphs are the spirits of air. They indicate a lightening of circumstances and the very real possibility that new ideas will increase your success and bring new opportunities. Since air is the element of communication, advertising, networking and other ways of getting out your message are very much favored at this point in the evolution of your project and the fulfillment of your wish/question.

There is also a possibility here that you will in due course receive a communication of significance concerning the issue that you are inquiring about. When this occurs has greatly to do with where you receive the Sylphs in the course of the oracle overall. If it is one of the grandparents, one of the first four, it is likely to come near the beginning of the enterprise. If it is one of the two parents, it will come toward the middle of the endeavor and if it is the child it will arrive near or at the completion of the project/question, which is to say the resolution of the issue.

This is also a good sign for the evocation of the Sylphs who are often conceived of as being the elementals of air who influence your project overall, which is to say help with the progression of this project in a positive way. Thus, evoke the air elementals to help you and bring fresh air and new ideas into the situation.

Mantra:

Va eronath altarli

Pronounced: Vah – e – rone – nayth ale – tayr (rhymes with pear) - lie

Meaning: To airy heights

Mudra:

Put the dominant hand in mudra two and the assisting hand in mudra four. Place the assisting hand elbow bent and outstretched fingers pointing toward the ceiling/sky, palm to the rear and have the dominant hand crossing the body so the outstretched fingers touch the wrist of the assisting hand, palm to body. Keeping the assisting hand in place, bring the dominant hand down in a scooping motion and then up so it is in the same position as the assisting hand on its side of the body, fingers up and palm toward the rear.

Visualization:

Red light outlined by bright purple

Chapter Thirty-Four: The Bucca

o
x
x
o
o
x
o

The Bucca are shapeshifters, sometimes appearing as horses, sometimes rabbits, or in fact in any form that they so choose. Thus this oracle concerns one's ability to adapt to various situations, individuals and social settings in such a way as to increase one's probability of success. Here the admonition is to become whom you need to be in order to achieve what you desire. If you insist on being one way in particular and refuse to adapt the situation will be much more difficult and the possibility of failure looms. However, that is not at all necessary. If you are willing to adjust to the circumstances you find yours'elf within the chances for success are greatly heightened.

Remember, in most cases, what you are changing here is not your essential s'elf but your personality, making it more pleasing and thus more influential. If you refine this art you will be able to influence nearly anyone, including the most obstinate and recalcitrant individuals and then success is surely guaranteed, if not in this particular project then surely overall.

When your personality becomes an expression of your soul, as it surely should be, then everyone will respond to it as being true and genuine and an authentic expression of your spirit and those who interact with you will know that they can trust you and even if you are eccentric and perhaps peculiar, as many elves are, people will know that you are real and will grow to accept you and respect you and from that great good fortune will come.

Mantra:

Ver ėld konjilosa

Pronounced: Veer eald (rhymes with felled) – lie cone – ji (rhymes with high) – low - sah

Meaning: In realms invisible

Mudra:

Have the dominant hand in mudra two and the assisting hand in mudra four. With elbow bent, have the assisting hand rest across the body and pointing toward the opposite shoulder, palm toward body. Have the dominant hand behind your back with palm away from body and bring it around to the front, circling down and across the body and then around and upward until, with palm toward the rear and elbow bent, it covers the assisting hand.

Visualization:

Luminous red light outlined by violet

Chapter Thirty-Five: The Menehunes

x
o
o
x
x
o
x

This is the sign of work and magic carried on unobtrusively, out of sight and out of mind. What others don't know, they can't obstruct. Let your magic be unseen in this situation, at this point, except as its effects manifest. Then everything shall proceed smoothly and all will turn out well.

There is also a certain socially conscious aspect to getting this sign. Be sure that what you are doing benefits more than yours'elf. If what you desire will also rebound to the good fortune of the community overall that is a definite plus in this situation and will make the possibilities of success even greater.

It is probable that you will have to work on this a little bit at a time. This oracle signifies a long-term magic that is achieved in increments. It is unlikely that you can put out energy once and have it all done. This is something that requires continual effort and even when completed most likely will require regular maintenance and periodic improvements. So be sure that you are in it for the long haul because this magic will require it of you.

Mantra:

La das u sol

Pronounced: Lah dace you soul

Meaning: By dark of night

Mudra:

Position the dominant hand in mudra five and the assisting hand in mudra seven, which is a fist. Have the assisting hand over your heart, palm toward body. Have the dominant hand by your side, palm to side, outstretched fingers toward floor/ground. Bring the dominant hand up in an arc so the top of the hand bumps the bottom of the assisting hand and then moves outward and forward the hand twisting as you do so, so that the palm turns upward, as though you are offering something.

Visualization:

Brilliant green light outlined by amber light

Chapter Thirty-Six: The Duendes

x
o
o
x
x
o
o

This is an oracle of the wee folk, the little folk, who may seem unimportant to many but who are in fact the little cogs that keep the whole world turning. They may not be famous or of high social standing, in fact, they are very unlikely to be so, but their efforts keep everything maintained and in order and without them the world would quickly grind to a standstill.

So in receiving this oracle it is important to pay attention to the details, to the small things and the people who often go unnoticed but are really a vital aspect of your success. They particularly need encouragement and if that comes not just in the form of compliments, which are very important, but in genuine rewards and incentives then that is all to the better. Whatever you give them will be returned many times in the benefits that are received from their daily efforts.

And remember that while they may not seem important individually that collectively they are very significant. If you can unite and organize their powers, truly great things can be accomplished. Remember also what the great masters know, which is that there is a place for everyone and no one's talents should be left to atrophy. Those who know how to inspire the wee folk, the Duendes, and fill them with enthusiasm will have great success and can fulfill all that they dream of and aspire toward.

Mantra:

Cha zil jugrym

Pronounced: Chah zile (rhymes with pile) jew - grim

Meaning: Each little detail

Mudra:

Place the dominant hand in position five and the assisting hand in position seven. Place the assisting hand so the fist is against the same side hip, palm toward rear, elbow out. Have the dominant hand so the outstretched fingers are across the body touching the elbow of the assisting hand, palm toward the rear. Leaving the assisting hand in place, bring the dominant hand up and across your eyes so it ends up with you peeking through the gap between the third finger and the pinkie finger.

Visualization:

Bright green light outlined by radiant brown

Chapter Thirty-Seven: The Huldu Folk

O
O
O
O
X
X
X

The Huldu Folk have the ability to shift dimensions and realms quite easily, slipping from one to another with ease. Getting this oracle is a sign that you need to increase your ability to move from one situation to another with facility so there is little or no stress for you in doing so. This is the sign of a need for increasing your competence at making transformations and shifting from one project to another with as little difficulty as possible. Thus this oracle is one for the multi-tasker and may very well be an indication that the fulfillment of this wish and the answer to the question you have asked of the oracle involves a variety of different skills and activities carried out one after the other and/or interchangeably.

This may also be a sign that there are times in the course of the development of this project that you will need to slip away, to rest and recuperate, and perhaps allow things to develop on their own without additional action or interference. Not everything can be achieved at once and knowing how to pace yours'elf without losing sight of your goals can be vital at times. Then you can return with renewed energy and zeal and continue to secure the success you desire.

This may also be an indication that you desire a safe and secure place to work undisturbed: a den, or private office, a cabin in the woods, whatever provides you with the seclusion and privacy you may need to work without interruption and to think and imagine without being constantly called to other things. At the same time, it just may be that you cannot leave the hubbub and turmoil of daily life and instead must find a way to concentrate on what you are doing while also dealing with kids, pets, colleagues or whatever. If you can deal with all this without falling apart or pulling your hair out and screaming, then you will surely be a great success.

Mantra:

Ciddas latenzard

Pronounced: Sid – dace lay – ten – zayrd (rhymes with fared_

Meaning: Stepping sidewise

Mudra:

Position the dominant hand in mudra four and the assisting hand in mudra eight. Have the assisting hand so it is over your mouth, palm to mouth and have the dominant hand so the outstretched fingers are touching the back of the assisting hand. Then bring the dominant hand outward and forward slowly until the outstretched fingers are pointing away from you, the palm downward.

Visualization:

Radiant purple light outlined by white

Chapter Thirty-Eight: The Ellyllon

o
o
o
o
x
x
o

This is a sign of wish fulfillment. In receiving the Ellyllon at least part of what you wish will come true. This is not to say that your entire goal will not be achieved, but that a part of what you desire, some part of the puzzle will fall into place shortly. The time involved has greatly to do with where you receive this sign in the oracle overall. If it is one of the grandparents, then it should occur relatively near the beginning. Thus if we thought that the project would take a year then getting this as a grandparent would make it likely that it would happen sometime in the first five or six months, depending on if it is the first, second, third or fourth grandparent. If it is received as a parent then it is likely to occur somewhere in the middle of the project and as the child then near the end or completion of the project. That is if you did this oracle before the project begin, otherwise, the timing is calculated according to when you did the oracle. The moment that you did and received the oracle in that case being regarded as the beginning and the calculation of when the wish may come true is from that origination point.

Of course, sometimes one simply doesn't know how long it will be until a goal/wish/desire is fulfilled and thus one has no measure with which to calculate. If that is the case, then if you receive this sign in the grandparents or parents you must simply wait until this part of the wish comes true and then figure out the probable time of the completion of the entire wish from that. Still, the important thing here is that this is a good sign and a real indication that the things you desire will in time be granted or achieved.

Mantra:

Kanili kivïn

Pronounced: Kay – nigh – lie kiv (rhymes if dive) - in

Meaning: Favors granted

Mudra:

The dominant hand should be in mudra four and the assisting hand in mudra eight. Have the assisting hand behind your back just above the waist, palm away from you. Have the dominant hand at your breastbone, palm downward, and move it slowly outward to its own side until the arm is extended fully, palm still down, outstretched fingers point out to the side away from you.

Visualization:

Brilliant purple light outlined by silver

Chapter Thirty-Nine: The Dooinney-Oie

x
x
o
o
o
o
x

This is an indication of what may be called the dark horse, which is to say an unseen and unexpected element that will affect this issue at the point in which the sign is received: in the grandparents, near the beginning to middle, the parents, the middle, and the child, near the end. This may also be an indication of the rise and success of the underdog. But essentially this means that it is unlikely that anyone, including you unless you heed this oracle, will see this one coming. However, it is still on the order of expect the unexpected, which is to say all you can do is prepare yours'elf for things turning out differently than you thought that they would but still have little notion of what that surprising element will be.

So all that you can do in this situation is know that there are surprising and unpredictable elements in motion that will affect the issue. Thus resilience and adaptability are highly recommended. Stay flexible. Don't let this unexpected development catch you flatfooted.

This is a sign of success if you are able to stay in the middle of the changes and not be thrown off by unforeseen developments or difficulties. If you greet this new person or event with an open heart and mind then things should go well for you. All you really need to do is be flexible enough to incorporate this new aspect into your overall plan and continue on toward your goal.

Mantra:

La tarsalun'na ols

Pronounced: Lah tayr (rhymes with hair) – sah –loon – nah oles (rhymes with holes)

Meaning: By moonlight's gaze

Mudra:

Start with the dominant hand in mudra eight and the assisting hand in mudra five. Have the assisting hand so it is about a foot in front of the body, palm toward body, outstretched fingers pointing at a forty-five degree angle to the body. Have the dominant hand behind the assisting hand, palm toward that hand, fingers upward, then use the dominant hand to push the assisting hand farther away from the body twisting the dominant hand as you do so, so that both hands end up at a greater distance from the body with fingers pointing directly away from it.

Visualization:

Luminous white light outlined by green light

Chapter Forty: The Tylweth Teg

x
x
o
o
o
o
o

In receiving this oracle it is an indication that something is in transition and one must adapt to the changing situation. Perhaps things are going to slow down or maybe obstacles will arise. What we know for sure is the situation as it has been is in the process of change and if you are ready and prepared to greet this change with a positive attitude all will go well. Remember, this is a cyclic change and things will in time change back again. Your ease in making the change, however, may very well affect how quickly the transition takes place and how easily it may change again. If you are on top of things, and roll with the punches, so to speak, all will go well in the long run.

Even if things are slowing down, and alas this is quite likely, there are still things that you may accomplish; and making the most of the time, even when the opportunities are limited, is very important. You may not be able to accomplish a great deal, but by doing all that you can in the situation, you optimize your chances for success.

Also, if there are those who are working with you, remember that you may serve as an example for them. Don't let hard times get you down or spin you into negativity and depression. Remember, your attitude greatly affects those who look up to you and depend upon you and when you set an example of fortitude and perseverance, those that follow your example will be hearten thereby.

Mantra:

La salun landas

Pronounced: Lah say – loon lane - dace

Meaning: By twilight dawning

Mudra:

Position the dominant hand in mudra eight and the assisting hand in mudra five. Have the assisting hand down by your side, palm toward side and the dominant hand, arm straight out from its shoulder, palm to the front. Bring both hands to shoulder height in front of you, palms toward each other, outstretched fingers pointing away from you.

Visualization:

Bright silver light outlined by green light

Chapter Forty-One: The Brown Man

x
o
x
o
o
x
x

The indication of this sign is that one is in an assisting position and is dependent upon someone else to take the lead or make a move before one is able to continue onward. Perhaps you are waiting for someone to make a decision, or for some paperwork to come through, or merely get around to doing what is needed so you may continue onward. It may seem that harassing them will get them going, but this is seldom the case. Most people are like mules and the more you push them the more they tend to resist. However, gentle and kindly reminders, plus gifts or the promise of personal incentives may help things along. The carrot often works much better than the stick.

In the meantime, focus your attention elsewhere, for there are surely things that you can do or prepare for doing once the situation is on the move again. Clean things up, clear the way, do whatever you can on your part to get things going and then rest with assurance that once the energy changes you will be ready to make the most of the opportunity when it presents itself.

And remember to encourage those around you, helping them to do their best and improve what they are doing, without undue criticism, for criticism even when it is well intentioned is often painful for sensitive souls struggling to succeed. Praise, with helpful hints usually are the best way to nurture others. Keep in mind the whole world is connected and by helping others you are helping yours'elf even if the link between the two actions are not direct or clear.

Mantra: La unka roth

Pronounced: Lah you-n (rhymes with June) – kay row-th

Meaning: By simple means

Mudra:

Place the dominant hand in mudra two and the assisting hand in mudra three. Have the assisting hand with outstretched fingers toward the floor/ground, palm against the front of your same side leg. Have the dominant hand to its same side, outstretched fingers to the ground/floor, palm against side of your leg. Keeping the assisting hand in place, bring the dominant hand upward in front of the body, make a loop about midway and then continue until the outstretched fingers are pointing toward opposite shoulder, palm to body.

Visualization:

Vibrant orange red light

Chapter Forty-Two: The Green Man

x
o
x
o
o
x
o

This oracle indicates taking direct action in the most simple and efficient way. It often indicates that there is confusion or a misunderstanding, perhaps even false rumors being spread and one must deal with these issues and quite possibly the person or persons responsible for them. It doesn't favor the dramatic or the flowery really, but rather it suggests taking actions that are impersonal or transpersonal and to the point. Do what is needed and nothing more. Don't make it personal. Be like a thunderstorm and clear the air and thus the way, and then everything will flower on its own and all will turn toward success.

This is the image of spring waking up from and overcoming winter. There may be a certain amount of uncertainty at first. One may wonder if it is a false spring and that some things will blossom forth only to be caught by frost later on. So proceed with a certain caution. You can be sure that the situation is moving in the right direction but don't overestimate your strength at this time or assume the weakness of those whom you may be called to deal with.

Ultimately, you are favored by the time, but a certain wise hesitation is best here. Probe the forces that you are confronting, find their true strength and the chink in their armor and then proceed with reason and measure. Overdoing your triumph is also to be avoided. Make what you do arise from necessity and nothing more and then the way will be opened and you can advance onward without the baggage that you would otherwise bear with you.

Mantra:

Ver aldar torp

Pronounced: Veer aldar tour-p

Meaning: In forest green

Mudra:

Place the assisting hand in mudra three and the dominant hand in mudra two. Position the assisting hand outstretched fingers pointing toward opposite side hip, palm to front of body. Have the dominant hand outstretched fingers on assisting hand's elbow, palm inward toward body. Slide the dominant hand downward, across the lower part of the assisting arm until the index finger of the dominant hand is just beyond and touching the middle finger of the assisting hand, both palms toward body.

Visualization:

Neon red outlined by orange light

Chapter Forty-Three: The Swan

x
o
o
x
o
x
x

Swans are often associated with the elven, particularly in the form of our swan ships (just as Vikings have their dragon ships). They are a symbol of beauty and elegance, as we elves are in popular lore and receiving this sign denotes that while there may not be anything of great significance that you can do to move things along or affect this situation at this point, that you may consider what the artistic, the beautiful and the creative may accomplish to increase your chances of success. Consider what you may do to make things more attractive, more enchanting. Remember that while you may not wish to judge a book by its cover that its cover may attract someone enough to check out what the contents actually are.

Elfin surely is based mostly upon the loving and caring relationships that we elves have for each other and yet, the beauty of our surroundings and our own attention to being as graceful and beautiful as we can be, enhances the wonder of our realm. This is the time for decorative flourishes. They are not the most important thing but they do add to the situation.

And remember, also, that swans, while they may be beautiful and graceful can be fierce if they need to be. But let's hope that it doesn't come to that and a smile and a bit of eloquence will have the effect you desire.

Mantra:

Yalandas darsh

Pronounced: Yeah – lane – dace dare-sh

Meaning: Expressing grace

Mudra:

Start with the dominant hand in mudra three and the assisting hand in mudra seven. Place the assisting hand with the bottom of the fist in the upturned palm of the dominant hand, so with elbows by your side it forms a triangle to your front. Keeping the hands together, bring them upward in an arc, as though you are pushing the assisting hand with the dominant hand, until the top of the assisting hand, the thumb and index finger are pressed against one's upper chest, with the palm of the dominant hand toward one's body.

Visualization:

Brilliant orange light outlined in bright amber

Chapter Forty-Four: The White Buffalo Woman

x
o
o
x
o
x
o

This symbol is a sign of grace, but not physical grace as is the case of the previous sign, but of the grace of the sacred and holy upon those who are pure of soul, mind and spirit. Thus in receiving this oracle know that you are being graced by the spirit and as long as you go forth with purity in your heart and an intention to do what is best for all concerned then success will be granted to you.

This is also a sign that things will be getting better for you. However, if you haven't already you may consider beginning to do the mantras and mudras that come with the seven oracles you have received (the other six and this one). This is particularly important in this case. In most of the others, it is up to you whether you wish to enact a ritual to heighten the possibility of success, but when you receive this sign it is a definite indication that it will further you to develop a practice of doing the rituals you evoked in this question until the goal you wish has been achieved to your satisfaction.

Also, there is a community orientation to this sign, so if you can recruit others to help you with this ritual, even if it is only sometimes, it will be even more effective. If, in fact, your question concerned relationship or group activities in some fashion, then this is an even stronger indication of ultimate success.

Mantra:

Eltar'na yer

Pronounced: Eel – tayr – na year

Meaning: Nature's way

Mudra:

Begin with the dominant hand in mudra three and the assisting hand in mudra seven. Have both hands by their respective sides, palms toward body. Bring them both up to the front of the body and tap the knuckles of the assisting hand into the palm of the dominant hand forming a triangle that is at a forty-five degree angle to the upper body.

Visualization:

Radiant brownish orange light

Chapter Forty-Five: The Bogies

x
o
o
o
o
o
x

This is a warning. There are certain individuals it is best not to have anything to do with for they will surely bring trouble in their wake and if you get involved with them the success of the issue about which you are inquiring becomes in doubt. Remember your mother probably told you to watch out for certain people who are bad company and in this case it is best if you heed her advice. It is true that sometimes our parents would scare us with tales of the Bogie man who would come if we didn't behave, but in this case the problem is that this individual won't scare you at first but will act friendly and then tempt you into things that will lead you into difficulties and when the going gets rough they will be gone leaving you to hold the bag. And if later you get a chance to confront them about their behavior they will just laugh at you and tell you that you made your own choice in the matter and you will know that this is so.

So, make the right choice from the very start and avoid these individuals like the plague. As exciting as they may seem, they don't have good intentions toward you, they only wish to use you and enjoy getting you in trouble. Do yours'elf a favor and ignore their enticements. If you can do that all will go well in the long run and everything you have hoped for will eventually turn out, if you can just be patient and wait. For one of the things these individuals tend to offer are shortcuts that are in fact too good to be true. Let that be your warning sign.

Mantra:

Kon tugli nectaïn

Pronounced: Cone two-g – lie neek- tah - in

Meaning: No strings attached

Mudra:

Position the dominant hand in mudra eight and the assisting hand in mudra seven. Have the dominant hand fingers toward ceiling/sky, palm toward rear, elbow bent, by its shoulder. Have the assisting hand, down by side, palm to rear. Move both hands at the same time so the dominant hand passes the assisting hand mid-body, and ends up fingers pointing toward floor/ground, palm still toward the rear, and assisting hand is now up, palm to rear, elbow bent, flat of the fist toward sky/ceiling.

Visualization:

Silver light outlined by amber

Chapter Forty-Six: The Unseelie

x
o
o
o
o
o
o

This sign is very similar to the previous one, although in that instance one is tempted to hang out with the wrong person while here the problem is most definitely from being in the wrong crowd, a group of individuals or a social setting that are just not conducive to your evolution and development as a soulful individual nor to the long term success of the question you are asking about.

Unfortunately, there is something intriguing about these folks, something that attracts you and draws you to them, and thus the dilemma. Still, if you wish to achieve your goals then your success depends upon finding those who are more in keeping with your soulful aspirations and who will nurture your spiritual elfin being. Alas, while you may wish to be with both groups, they simply don't mix and you will have to make a decision about what you truly wish for your life and your future.

This is often the problem that confronts the newly awakened elfin. Those that we knew as friends and who have been one's close social network will not accept this new understanding that we elves have of our elven s'elves. In time, the elf must choose between pursuing the Elven Way (see our book of that title) or falling back into the comfortable habits of life as sHe was used to it being. In deciding to pursue one's spiritual path, one often feels lonely, but in time one finds those that are really meant for one and one discovers that one gave up something transitory for something that will have positive affects on one's life for lifetimes to come.

Mantra:

Tat tae emat rudlu el

Pronounced: Tate tay e – mate rude – lou eel

Meaning: As the mood takes me

Mudra:

Begin with dominant hand in mudra eight and assisting hand in mudra seven. Elbow bent and down at side have the assisting hand across body just under ribcage, palm toward body. Have the dominant hand so the pointy part of its elbow is resting in the lacuna formed by the thumb and index finger of the assisting hand, while the hand is flat against the opposite shoulder, palm inward. Bring the dominant hand downward across the body until it is by its own side, fingers pointed toward floor/ground, palm toward rear.

Visualization:

Luminous white light outlined by amber

Chapter Forty-Seven: The Phoenix

o
o
o
o
o
x
x

Just when you thought that all was lost, things make a turn for the better and the energy begins moving again. Those who were obstructing you fall out of your way, tangled in their own webs of deceit or simply wandering off to make complications for someone else, bored with you now. This is all to the better and things will begin again, although somewhat slowly at first, like healing from a sickness, or perhaps, just waking up in the morning. Give yours'elf time to stretch and get your head in order before you attempt any serious efforts, but be assured you can now take action with greater certainty of success and if you continue resolutely all will turn out well.

This is in a sense a rebirth, a revival after what seemed to be a failure. But there were still embers glowing deep within and in the depth of your being you never gave up and thus the spirits didn't abandon you either. You may have thought that it was all over but now they come seeking you, urging you to try again, and you may heed them without reluctance for a new era is indeed dawning and the possibilities are increasing.

Perseverance and steadfast resolve in proceeding will aid things to turn out well and in the end you may achieve more than you originally imagined.

So despair not, nor overly hesitant be, yet rush not either, but step by step gauge the energy and do all that you can within reason, overcoming every obstacle as it arises until success is achieved. Resting when needed, proceeding onward as the time dictates, confident that the spirits support you and the achievement of your goal is in sight.

Mantra:

An hemali luftïn

Pronounced: Ane he – mah – lie louft (rhymes with goofed) – in

Meaning: From ashes risen

Mudra:

Position the dominant hand in mudra two and the assisting hand in mudra eight. Have the assisting hand so the elbow is at your side and the lower arm straight out, fingers pointed away from you, palm toward opposite side. Have the dominant hand up near your same side cheek, palm toward cheek and then bring it down and across the assisting hand, the outstretched fingers touching the palm of the assisting hand as it passes, as though striking a match, and bringing it down to settle in front of one's same side leg, outstretched fingers pointed downward.

Visualization:

Brilliant red light outlined by white

Chapter Forty-Eight: The Bennu

o
o
o
o
o
x
o

The Bennu bird of ancient Egyptian origin (see Nicholas de Vere, the Dragon Legacy or Laurence Gardner, the Realm of the Ring Lords for the connection between the Ancient Egyptians and the Elves) is sometimes thought to be the inspiration for the Phoenix, but the Bennu (sometimes spelled Benu) is self created. His is a sign not merely of reincarnation, of rising from the ashes, but of arising in the first place, of s'elf becoming. Thus he is a symbol for most elven folk who must lift thems'elves up out of what is, for the most part, a cultural desert for our people, with little of our heritage left to go on and that mostly in the way of fiction much of which is erroneous or biased by the culture it is derived from or appealing to.

Thus this oracle indicates that one must take the lead in this situation. To create something from seeming nothing, to step into realms uncharted and to call back to others, who are most likely hesitant and uncertain, to accompany you forward. If you are waiting for someone else to take the first step in these circumstances, you may be waiting a very long time. Make a move yours'elf and you will not regret it. Don't worry about the way things have been done previously. Don't question whether you are doing it right according to ancient formulas or popular belief. Take that step, do it as best you may, let your intuition and creative instincts guide you, become an Initiate and initiate.

Don't let the fact that others may not immediate approve or pick up on what you are doing deter you. Those who create new pathways are often criticized by those who fear to wander from the socially accepted ways. Simply do what you feel is best for yours'elf and all others and in time the wisdom of your path will become clear or you, yours'elf, will go from that to an even better way. Anyway you look at it, however, this is a good sign and a true step forward toward achieving your goals.

Mantra:

Daend sasnana

Pronounced: Day – eend (rhymes with fiend) says – nay - nah

Meaning: Born again

Mudra:

Position the dominant hand with mudra two and the assisting hand with mudra eight. Have the assisting hand, elbow bent at side, parallel to the floor/ground, palm down, at the forty-five degree angle to the body. Have the dominant hand downward at the front of the same side leg, palm to body and bring it upward, twisting so the palm turns toward the ceiling/sky and it bumps into and is stopped by the assisting hand, so that the palm of the assisting hand is over the heel and wrist of the dominant hand.

Visualization:

Bright red light outlined in white

Chapter Forty-Nine: The Gnomes

X
X
X
O
O
X
X

Gnomes have ever been a symbol of knowledge, often deep secret knowledge and arcane wisdom. In modern times they are often portrayed as woodsy farmer types, but in ancient days they were seen as esoteric librarians and keepers of the hidden and occult keys. In getting this oracle, it is a sign that there are secrets and techniques that will be revealed to you that may help you with this project/goal, although you may have to do a little research. It is surely a good sign for it denotes the power of small and seemingly unimportant things, like ideas, to have profound impact upon your life and the lives of others.

In searching for the hints that can help you further along this path you don't necessarily need to seek the advice of those who are noted and famous, but those folks, who may seem quite plain and modest really, who have some true experience and knowledge in the area that intrigues you.

If your question concerns money or worldly success then this sign indicates that steady work unobtrusively carried on will lead to success. If your question concerns relationship or romance the answer here is that modesty, loyalty and faithfulness are much to be desired. If you can demonstrate those aspects of character this will heighten your possibilities of a successful outcome.

There is also an element here that indicates that whatever you learn concerning this situation may come as a surprise to you and alter your outlook in terms of your desires. It may well be that you will discover that what you thought you wanted isn't what you really desire at all.

Mantra:

Kenas zard

Pronounced: key – nace zayrd (rhymes with faired)

Meaning: Knowing wise

Mudra:

Start with the dominant hand in mudra two and the assisting hand in mudra one. Have the two hands down by their respective sides and then bring them up until their outstretched fingertips touch, elbows bent, just under your chin, palms toward each other, as though you are praying or are in deep contemplation.

Visualization:

Radiant red light outlined in gold

Chapter Fifty: The Djinn

x
x
x
o
o
x
o

The Djinn are spirits that are sometimes called genies, and thus they are related from this both to the idea of the daemon (Greek, guiding and inspiring spirit) and to the concept and reality of genius. You certainly wish to evoke your own genius in dealing with this issue, to engage and challenge your creative nature and look at the question you are asking of this oracle once again in a fresh light. It is clear in getting this sign that you have something more to contribute to the situation that will increase your possibilities of success and heighten the potentiality of an outcome in keeping with what you have envisioned.

You may also wish to evoke a spirit to aid with this project. Try to get a spirit whose expertise is in the area that you are inquiring about (see our books An Elfin Book of Spirits and The Shining Ones [this one especially if you are looking for your own personal genie]). If you do so, allow these experts to do what they do best without micromanaging their efforts. Set them to the task and except for acknowledging them and feeding them periodically, trust in their expertise. Djinn, by the way, are spirits of fire and air primarily, which is to say energy and spirit, so keep that in mind when dealing with them. Burning candles for them can be very helpful.

While receiving this sign can indicate that you need some assistance to achieve your stated or desired goal, don't forget that you are the director of this magic. A djinn might be more powerful than you (and surely is), just as a doctor or dentist has the expertise to do what you cannot do for yours'elf, still you are the one in command. Therefore make sure your desires are clearly stated and cannot be misconstrued. They may be the experts, but you are the boss.

Mantra:

Lazdas ilu

Pronounced: Laze – dace eye - lou

Meaning: Burning bright

Mudra:

Put the dominant hand in mudra two and the assisting hand in mudra one. Place both hands so elbows are bent, outstretched fingers toward the ceiling/sky as though you are holding a revolver in each hand, then bring the hands forward so they are about ninety degrees from the body and give a little snap at the end as though you are cracking a whip.

Visualization:

Vibrant red light outlined in yellow

Chapter Fifty-One: The Centaur

X
O
O
X
X
X
X

The Centaur is a magical (some would say mythical) being of two worlds or two species blended together. Thus the Centaur is a sign of compromise particularly between two distinct peoples, races, or cultures, or even worlds, a blending of the magical world and the mundane world, the astral and the material, the human and the creature world. Thus getting this sign indicates that some compromise may be needed to further you on the path to achieving your goal. Thus a willingness to compromise, to adapt to changing circumstances is advised.

This oracle may also indicate that you will find assistance regarding this issue coming from someone who is from a different social group, someone who is not a part of your usual circle of friends. Treat this individual with respect and good fortune will come from this. Prejudice limits our intelligence and arbitrarily refusing the help of those who could further us just because they are different is pure ignorance (like cultures that don't educate women and thus deprive themselves of their genius). Don't assume but listen carefully and learn all that you can from everyone you encounter and the spirits will speak through them suggesting the pathways to follow that will lead to success.

Since a centaur is usually pictured as being half horse, the idea of travel is also indicated here and it is possible that the resolution to the question lies in travel or is to be found in a distant place or culture. Keep your mind alert and follow the signs and you will be guided toward a positive outcome.

Mantra:

Vyrlan tae telth

Pronounced: Ver – lane tay teal-th

Meaning: Between the worlds

Mudra:

Have the dominant hand in mudra one and the assisting hand in mudra position seven. Place the assisting hand over your navel, with palm toward body. Put the dominant so it is above the assisting hand and the two outstretched fingers are over and resting on the back of the assisting hand. Now tap those two fingers twice upon that hand.

Visualization:

Golden light outlined by amber light

Chapter Fifty-Two: The Satyr

x
o
o
x
x
x
o

If you receive this sign then you may encounter some old goat in dealing with this situation. This person may or may not have information that will be helpful to you, but will certainly act as though sHe does either way. If you are wise you will listen politely, thank the person for hir assistance (whether the advice was germane or not), consider it well (in case sHe actually knows what sHe is talking about) and continue on your way, incorporating this information into your plan or not as needed.

Most advice we receive is, of course, utterly useless. Some people don't know what they are talking about, many just want to sound like they are knowledgeable, some people just want to make a comment on the situation that makes no difference one way or another but occasionally someone actually says something that will prove helpful. Even if what this person says isn't directly related to the topic or even seems to be of use, consider that the spirits sometimes send us signs in unusual ways and though peculiar people. This is particularly relevant if you have asked for a sign or an omen. Then it is a matter of interpreting what the person says, much in the way that you would puzzle out the meaning of a dream.

If indeed you are looking for a sign or a message from the spirit world then you especially wish to note what those who are not quite normal, who are in certain ways not entirely human, may say to you, even in passing. Mostly, getting the Satyr indicates that a message is coming, listen to those who may strike you as a bit odd for they are often the voice of the spirit world.

Mantra:

La nyl caltomïn

Pronounced: Lah nil cal – tome - in

Meaning: By song evoked

Mudra:

Begin with the dominant hand in mudra one and the assisting hand in mudra seven. Have the assisting hand over your stomach, palm toward body and have the dominant over it, outstretched fingers toward opposite side. Leaving the assisting hand in place, bring the dominant hand up to your forehead and touch it with the outstretched fingers and then flip them slightly forward as though giving someone a lighthearted and casual salute or acknowledgement.

Visualization:

Yellow amber light

Chapter Fifty-Three: The Faun

X
O
O
O
O
X
X

The Faun may indicate that there is someone with a lot of energy but little knowledge or experience who is willing to help you in terms of this question. Using this energy correctly, which is to say finding something that they can do that won't interfere with or complicate what is already going on may be a bit of a challenge. They mean well but they are just not competent. Still, there must be something they can do.

At the same time, be cautious of those who wish to plunge in and do something without guidance or advice. These individuals inevitably make a mess of things. However, controlling their restless energy can be a bit of a chore. They often act with great authority as though they actually know what they are doing but it isn't long before they break something or, in fact, hurt thems'elves. Alas, sometimes the only thing you can do is to watch them make a fool of themselves and wait until they acknowledge it for they just won't listen to reason.

It is in fact best if you can spot them from the beginning and prevent them from acting at all or channel their energy into something that is harmless or something that, if things go wrong, will be only a minor inconvenience. At any rate, this is not a very good sign in that sense and often the most you can do is to minimize the potential damage.

Mantra:

Ena tylfverfel costa

Pronounced: E – nah till-f – veer – feel coss - tah

Meaning: With youthful vigor

Mudra:

Position the dominant hand in mudra two and the assisting hand in mudra seven. Have the assisting hand against your chest at the solar plexus and place the dominant hand so the three outstretched fingers are against and resting between the four fingers of the fist of the assisting hand. Move both hands slowly but determinedly forward away from the body.

Visualization:

Bright reddish amber light

Chapter Fifty-Four: The Abbey Lubbers

x
o
o
o
o
x
o

In getting this sign, you may be dealing with those who are quite nice and pleasant to be around but who don't really want to do much of anything other than tempt you away from your goal and your efforts to attain what you desire so that you will party with them. Alas, they don't take your goals seriously. These individuals are in many ways like the people who stand around and watch people work at building sites; only these individuals will also tempt you to abandon your work to go off and do something else. The question is, how badly do you wish to obtain this goal and how hard are you willing to work at it. It is true that we all need rest and relaxation sometimes. Almost no problem can be resolved simply by brute force and endless effort. Most great inspirations have come in moments when the inventor/creator, after having worked ceaseless for a long period, suddenly takes a break and has that eureka moment.

However, remember such moments cannot be forced and as Thomas Edison said, "Genius is one percent inspiration, ninety-nine percent perspiration." You need to put in that ninety-nine percent otherwise that inspiration is unlikely to be forthcoming. And those individuals who are ever tempting you away from your creative efforts are not helping. So be cautious. Be sure your work is done. Be sure that you have done all that you can to bring your vision to fruition and having done so you can then surely take a break and let the spirits do their part.

Mantra:

Inkurdurli dydonïn

Pronounced: Ine – coo – dur – lie did – doan - in

Meaning: Temptations denied

Mudra:

Start with the dominant hand in mudra two and the assisting hand in mudra seven. Have the assisting hand across the body, fist pointing to opposite shoulder, palm toward body. Place the dominant hand so it is out to the side, palm toward the front at the forty-five degree angle to the body, outstretched fingers pointing downward to the ground/floor about four feet from body. Keeping the assisting hand in place, bring the dominant hand upward until it is crossing the arm of the assisting hand, palm toward body.

Visualization:

Bright red light outlined by amber light

Chapter Fifty-Five: The Knockers

o
x
x
x
x
o
x

The Knockers or Tommy Knockers were said to warn miners (dwarves) of potential dangers, rather like the canary in the mine. Therefore, getting this oracle is a sign to watch out for possible difficulties ahead. Look out for the warning signs and heed all indications that there may be trouble brewing. If you are wise and ready you can avoid most of these problems before they occur with timely preventive measures. The point at which these troubles are likely to arise may be figured out by where you receive this sign in the series of oracles. If it is a grandparent it is likely to come near the beginning or before the first half. If a parent, it will be near the middle or just beyond. If you receive it as the child then they are likely to come near the end just as your wish seems about to be fulfilled.

It is important to realize that although these spirits bring you forewarning of problems that they are not the cause of the difficulties, in fact, they are acting on your behalf and endeavoring to aid you to avoid difficulties. Be sure to thank the spirits for their assistance and make some offerings to reward them. Appreciation, particularly in terms of real energy, is always well received.

Remember, don't ignore the signs or things will get even worse. Timely precautions will serve to make all things work out well.

Mantra:

La kreonïn setdas

Pronounced: Lah cree – ohn – in seat - dace

Meaning: With advanced warning

Mudra:

Position the dominant hand in mudra five and the assisting hand in mudra four. Have both hands at the bottom of your ribs on each side, palms toward body, elbows pointing out the back like lowered wings. Bring both hands directly forward, pointing to the front, twisting the hands as you do so, so that the palms are now downward.

Visualization:

Radiant green light outlined in purple

Chapter Fifty-Six: The Spriggans

o
x
x
x
x
o
o

In receiving this oracle, it is a sign that there will be difficulties at the point in the oracle series where this one appears. However, that you will encounter problems is not the major emphasis of this sign, for that in many ways is simply taken for granted. The point here is that you may overcome these difficulties in a step-by-step fashion. If you attempt to solve everything at once you are unlikely to succeed and more than likely will feel overwhelmed by all that confronts you. However, by applying yours'elf to one part of the problem at a time and merely keeping your head above water, so to speak, most of the troubled waters will recede on their own and everything will return to, if not normal, at least elfin typical, which is to say, unusual but fine. The advice here is to merely keep things going and don't succumb to the chaos that this time represents.

Spriggans are in many ways just wee folk and not of great power individually, but with cooperation and concerted effort they will serve to help you shore things up until the situation clears up entirely. At any rate, don't give up. This is only a temporary hassle and things will be progressing again shortly. Keep your spirits up and continue onward. The progress will surely be slow, but it is just this fact that will help you ultimately achieve what you desire.

It is possible that you will feel abandoned. That you and your spirits, your spriggans in this case, are all alone trying to keep things from falling apart when no one else seems to care. Don't let this fact get to you. You are an elfin being, unique and individual and so naturally you will often be progressing into the unknown on your own. Be strong, hang on, and things will stabilize again in time and all will be well.

Mantra:

Ver elan tyltål

Pronounced: Veer e – lane till - tahl

Meaning: In ancient wonder

Mudra:

Put the dominant hand in mudra five and the assisting hand in mudra four. With elbows bent at sides, place the assisting hand a bit out from the body at stomach height with the palm facing upward. Have the dominant hand just above it with the palm facing downward toward the assisting hand. Now, flip their position so the assisting hand is on top and the dominant hand beneath.

Visualization:

Neon green light outlined by violet light

Chapter Fifty-Seven: The Each Uisges

o
x
o
o
x
o
x

These are dangerous times and you are dealing with some potentially dangerous individuals; however, if you are wise and don't panic you can gradually extricate yours'elf from the situation and if you are very wise and a bit clever you may even be able to turn this situation to your advantage. The Each Uisges are dangerous beings but they can be harnessed so that their dangerous energy can serve to protect you. It was probably Each Uisges that swept away the Dark Riders when they attempted to cross the river into Rivendell in the Lord of the Rings.

Getting this oracle is surely not a good sign, nor a sign of success, however, if you are careful in proceeding and venture no farther than necessary to keep out of danger, then all should be well. Just remember, don't panic, don't run, stay calm. These creatures are like dogs, if they sense fear they will go after you. Stay strong, make no sudden moves, and even if you don't feel courageous, don't let it show.

Keep in mind that all that is really necessary in this situation is to keep your cool and don't do anything to make things worse. If you can hang on and keep moving slowly forward, everything should turn out to your advantage in the long run. This is just one oracle among seven and it is the combination and their relationships that can lead to success in time.

Mantra:

La quant kafaïn

Pronounced: Lah que – aint kay – fah - in

Meaning: By water protected

Mudra:

Put both the dominant and the assisting hand in mudra six. With elbows bent have both hands out toward the front, outstretched fingers toward the ceiling/sky, palms toward body, as though you are at a heavy metal concert. Then, turn both hands down so the outstretched fingers are pointing toward the floor/ground, as though giving a thumbs down sign only with mudra six.

Visualization:

Bright deep blue light

Chapter Fifty-Eight: The Sluagh

o
x
o
o
x
o
o

You definitely wish to avoid these beings if you can, or limit contact as much as possible. This is decidedly a sign of trouble but things can turn out well in the end if you are cautious and bide your time. There is no way to get out of this immediately and to attempt to do so is most likely to make things worse. However, great care is advised and if you are patient the problems will pass on their own.

The Sluagh are dangerous folk and you do not wish to be involved with them under any circumstances. At the same time, if you do run into them, try to keep contact to a minimum. Be respectful, but not obsequious. They are violent and unpredictable, but courtesy is appreciated by all people as long as it isn't forced. Be strong but not threatening. Keep to yours'elf as much as possible. Mind your own business and wait until the danger passes. They are restless types and are inclined to go off on their own if you don't engage them. You may leave their presence but quietly and without haste so they do not notice you. Of course, it is best if you can avoid such beings altogether, but sometimes life puts us in situations that we did not ask for or anticipate so all you can do is your best, accept your fate and await the signs from the spirits that will guide you to safety.

Keep in mind the key here is patience, caution and keeping a low profile. In this situation being invisible or part of the woodwork is a good thing. Use your elven social camouflage skills and you will fade into the background until you can disappear from the scene altogether. Best of luck.

Mantra:

Wyl otwa kerohaïn

Pronounced: Will oat – wah key – row – hah - in

Meaning: All danger averted

Mudra:

Position both hands in mudra six. Place both hands, elbows bent, at the opposite shoulders, so the palms are toward body, the back of the thumbs touching the shoulder and the outstretched fingers protruding at an angle beyond the shoulder. Slide both hands down the arms until the protruding fingers are resting just above the elbow of the opposite arm, palms still inward toward body.

Visualization:

Deep blue light outlined by light blue

Chapter Fifty-Nine: Star-Fire

x
o
x
x
o
x
x

Receiving Star-Fire is a truly good sign and one that instills great luck and energy into you and this situation. Have faith in the magic of your elven stars and keep on, and through slow and steady work and gradual development everything will progress as it is meant to. This sign is a blessing, but in many ways it is a quiet blessing rather than a demonstrative one. It speaks of endurance and fortitude and the power to continue onward when others have abandoned the course. Your steadfastness will be rewarded in the end and you will be shown to have been right all along. You just need to continue onward undeterred by any obstacles or challenges you encounter on the way and politely ignore all naysayers and those whose pessimistic outlooks and negative forecasts are designed to get you to give up.

Lift your arms toward the sky, draw in the magical energy of the Star-Fire, let it settle into your soul and arouse your spirit. You are elven born, star born, one of the ancients reborn into this world and are aided and guided by the Shining Ones. Remember your true destiny and your true nature. And remember your mission. If the question you are inquiring of the oracle isn't directly about this purpose then it surely is indirectly so, for the elven all paths lead to Elfin and we are here to create it wherever we are. Journey onward, kindred, the stars are shining upon you.

Mantra:

Lawath'na ols

Pronounced: Lay – wayth'nah olss (rhymes with holes)

Meaning: Destiny's gaze

Mudra:

Begin with both hands in mudra three. Have the hands together, palms facing each other, so the outstretched fingers are touching at their tips creating a cone shape in front of your nose, as though praying, and thumbs touching as well. Then separate the hands, each toward its own side, turning them inward so they wind up facing toward the rear and one's shoulders.

Visualization:

Neon orange light

Chapter Sixty: The Silver Flame of Elfin

x
o
x
x
o
x
o

The Sacred Silver Flame burns in Elfin keeping all our true names within its blazing fires and guiding us all homeward to our true s'elves and our true natures. In receiving this oracle, it is time to consider your goal in regard to the question you have asked of the oracle as it concerns your fate and your destiny. How does achieving this goal, this desire, further your purpose and evolution as a soulful and spiritual being? If the realization of this issue doesn't actually further you, than why are you pursuing it? What is the course you should be taking? What will foster your evolution?

This sign is a call from the Shining Ones to pay attention to what is truly important for you and for your kindred. There is a mission for you if you are willing to accept it. Pay attention to the omens that appear around you, heed your dreams; there is a message coming for you soon to guide you to what you are really meant to do. Remember, the resolution of this issue isn't about the question itself but your destiny through the lifetimes. See your life in terms of centuries and aeons. Where are you headed in the long run? Who are you becoming? Who do you truly wish to be? The Sacred Silver Flame of Elfin is burning and it ever holds your true name in the warmth of its embrace calling you home to Elfin.

Mantra:

Eldanalla med

Pronounced: Eel – day – nail – lah mead

Meaning: Eternally bound

Mudra:

Begin with both hands in mudra three. Position them with thumbs against forehead, outstretched fingertips touching and fingers upward as though creating a triangular crown, then bring both hands down, turning them inward so they end up with the palms to rear and upper arms straight out and forward from the shoulders, bend elbows so lower arms are at a ninety degree angle to the upper arms, and outstretched fingers pointing toward the ceiling/sky. Note that this movement is almost identical to the previous one, except that it begins and ends with the hands and arms in a higher position.

Visualization:

Deep orange light outlined by bright orange

Chapter Sixty-One: The Ganconer

o
x
x
x
o
o
x

The Ganconer is the love-talker, but we need to realize that this sign isn't merely about romance (although if the question you asked of the oracle was about love, romance or relationship then this is a really good omen) but is about the ability to influence individuals particularly though the use of a charming and persuasive personality. Is this you? Do you have the type of personality that inclines people to assist you just because they like you? If so, then now is the time to use this ability. If not, then it is likely that a person of this sort will be coming into the picture soon and influencing the situation. Keep a lookout for this individual at the time that this sign appears in the series of the seven oracles you have drawn.

This may also be an indication that it is time to increase the power of your personality. This can be done by consistency of character, by keeping your word and your promises (always important for a magician of any sort but particularly elven magicians) and making your actions live up to your pronouncements, which is to say that it is important to walk your talk, put your money where your mouth is, and rid yours'elf of hypocrisy in all of its forms.

Increasing the power of your personality, so that individuals respect you even if they don't like or agree with you, is an important development for the elven magician and is a key to elven enchantment (see our books the Keys to Elfin Enchantment). Do all you can to make yours'elf strong, not merely of body but of mind, spirit and soul as well.

Mantra:

Joul elaf lyrodur

Pronounced: Jo – yule e – layf lur (as in lurid) – row - dur

Meaning: Through gentle persuasion

Mudra:

Start with the dominant hand in mudra seven and the assisting hand in mudra four. Have the dominant hand so the arm is forward and out from the shoulder and the palm is downward toward floor/ground. The assisting hand should be across the body with the outstretched fingers resting on the arm of the dominant hand just above the elbow. Keeping the assisting hand in place, pull the dominant hand back toward the body, twisting as you do so, so that the palm comes upward to the ceiling/sky, the elbow protrudes out from the back, and the assisting hand, while staying in place, is caused to end up with the outstretched fingers on the upturned inner wrist of the dominant hand.

Visualization:

Bright amber light outlined by purple light

Chapter Sixty-Two: The Enchanters

o
x
x
x
o
o
o

At this point in the proceedings, we are called to consider the presentation. It is not the essential thing, but it can make a big difference. It is not the meaning of the message; it is just the cover and not the contents of the book, but to attract readers it may help if the cover is beautiful or intriguing. So it is at this juncture that we need to examine how we are presenting/advertising the goal that we are working toward. As we say, this is not the essential thing; we have all surely encountered products, such as movies, whose commercials were actually better than the product itself. But while not neglecting what is important, making what we desire as attractive as possible will certainly help, particularly if we desire to recruit others to aid us as well as heightening our own continuing interest as things develop.

It is also possible in receiving this oracle that someone will come along to either enliven the process or potentially lure you away to other interests. A question may arise about whether you really wish to continue to pursue this course or not. It may be that something more fascinating will arise and you will need to consider whether all the energy you have invested in this project thus far will be abandoned, and potentially wasted.

In the long run, it is up to you. What do you really desire? Whatever it is, be sure to make it as interesting and exciting as you can. Enchantment is life and heals and revives all who experience it.

Mantra:

La eltarvar chanadur

Pronounced: Lah eel – tayr (like tar in tarry) – vayr (like var in vary) chay – nay - dur

Meaning: By natural attraction

Mudra:

Position the dominant hand in mudra seven and the assisting hand in mudra four. Have the arms crossed over your chest so the assisting arm is over the dominant arm and the outstretched fingers are resting on and just above the elbow of the dominant arm, while the dominant arm crosses under the assisting arm but the dominant hand, the fist, is on and above the elbow of the assisting arm. Now, leaving the assisting arm in place, bring the dominant hand and arm out from under the assisting arm and upward and thump your opposite side shoulder with that fist.

Visualization:

Brilliant amber light outlined by violet light

Chapter Sixty-Three: The Fair Folk

o
o
x
x
x
o
x

Usually when we speak of the Fair Folk, one of the many names for the Elfae, the elven and faerie peoples, we are given to consider that our peoples are beautiful or fair. Sometimes, it is said that this name is used, as are some others, in a flattering or hopeful way, so as not to offend us (for not all fae are beautiful in a physical sense and some, even when they are beautiful can, none-the-less, be quite terrifying). But these elves also consider this term with the idea that we are fair folk, which is to say we do what is fair and just for all peoples. So in getting this oracle, you are urged to consider what is truly fair in this situation. Is what you desire fair for everyone? Is the way you are going about achieving it fair as well? Your success may not depend upon these questions but your ultimate good fortune and the evolution of your soulful spirit very much does.

From the point of view of the elves, fairness in terms of beauty of form is connected in the long run to fairness of spirit, by which we mean treating all beings fairly. As we live our lives in a fair fashion, being just/fair in all that we do, we develop an integrity that accrues to our physical being. We become, through our actions and through the lifetimes, more and more fair in a physical fashion. The opposite is also true. Those who abandon fairness of spirit are in time in danger of losing fairness of form through the course of their lives and their lifetimes.

So, in this situation, seek what is fair in every sense and in doing that you will bring about good fortune for yours'elf and all others and everything will turn out well.

Mantra:

Yalanïn ena elådanara

Pronounced: Yeah – lane – in e – nah e – lah – day – nair - rah

Meaning: Expressed with elegance

Mudra:

Place the dominant hand in mudra five and the assisting hand in mudra two. Have the arms crossed, dominant arm over assisting arm, so that each hand is pointing toward the opposite shoulder, palms toward body. Then, leaving the assisting hand in place, bring the dominant hand so the elbow is bent, the palm toward rear and the outstretched fingers pointing toward ceiling/sky in front of its shoulder. Then bring that hand down so that its outstretched fingers are pointing to the ground/floor but the palm is still to rear.

Visualization:

Neon green light outlined by vibrant red

Chapter Sixty-Four: The People of Peace

O
O
X
X
X
O
O

Like the appellation of Fair Folk, the title People of Peace is one that was used often in a rather hopeful fashion, seeking to flatter and appease us. It is hoped that we will be peaceful and to fill other individual's lives with peace instead of meddling in ways that wind up making them miserable. So the question here is how can you bring yours'elf and this situation into harmony and in doing so further your progress toward your goal? And how can you bring others involved into a harmonious relationship with yours'elf and with each other so everything will become as it is meant to be, as you've envisioned it and as you desire?

It should also be clear that in drawing this oracle that force is to be avoided. Peaceful progress is the key to lasting success. Using force will only create resistance, which is exactly what you don't wish to have or increase at this time. The idea here is to grease the wheels so to speak, to get out the social WD40 (not a lubricant as some folks think but a solvent), and also oil the parts that seem to be grinding together. If you can do that all will go smoothly and you will be closer to obtaining what you desire without constant and continual interference.

At the same time, be at peace. It could be that there is nothing you can do but be patient. Having done all that you can, and perhaps having come to the conclusion that some of the individuals involved simply will not change the way they are, then be at peace within your own s'elf. If you can't change the world around you, transform your own nature and in doing that you will have created changes on the planes of spirit that will in time transform the world. Meditate and wait. Further developments will come in their own time.

Mantra:

Joul olytu

Pronounced: Jo – yule oh – lit – two

Meaning: Through diplomacy

Mudra:

Begin with the dominant hand in mudra position five and the assisting hand in mudra position two. Have the arms crossed at the wrists, with the assisting wrist over the dominant wrist, beneath your navel, palms inward toward body, outstretched fingers pointing downward and off to opposite side. Keeping the assisting hand in place, and keeping the wrists in contact, bring the dominant hand under and up and over the assisting arm until the hands are in essentially the same position as they began but with the dominant wrist over the assisting wrist.

Visualization:

Luminous green light outlined by dark red

Chapter Sixty-Five: The Hidden Folk

x
x
x
x
o
o
x

In getting the Hidden Folk, one is reminded that some things are best done in secret and out of the public view. Those things that people don't know about they can't obstruct. So the idea here is to proceed with a bit of introversion. Keep your secrets to yours'elf and continue onward without drawing any attention to yours'elf or your desires concerning this issue.

Of course, it is also possible that there are others who are acting in secret whose actions will affect the outcome of your question. There is little that you may do about this fact except to remain aware that this is a possibility and remain flexible and adaptable, ready to deal with any unexpected turns of fate that may arise. You need not assume that this is necessarily a bad thing. These individuals may not be acting directly against you, in fact, it is most likely that they are merely pursuing their own interests and are not at present aware that they will affect your desires at all. Under such circumstances, you may think that you should reveal what you are doing or your desired outcome, but again you are cautioned against doing so. Simply keep the possibility of people acting at cross purposes to you in your awareness and be ready to adjust your actions and your strategy accordingly. If you have a bit of elven far sight, then it is possible you may proceed in such a way as to avoid conflict altogether.

If you cannot, then compromise under such circumstances is greatly advised. Avoid any confrontation that may develop as much as possible and seek a solution that works for everyone. Be patient and be aware that this is probably just an accidental and temporary obstruction and bide your time and things shall work out in the long term, although perhaps not quite as quickly as you first hoped.

Mantra:

La dartlynli murfendo

Pronounced: Lah dare-t – lynn – lie muir – feen - doe

Meaning: By forces undetected

Mudra:

Start with the dominant hand in mudra seven and the assisting hand in mudra one. Have both arms bent at elbow with hands upward so they are toward the ceiling/sky, palms to the rear on respective sides. Turn the palms inward toward your body and bring the hands downward and forward, elbows still at your sides, and about midway loop the hands down and around so they end up with the palms toward the sky/ceiling and the hands about waist height and to the front of the body.

Visualization:

Amber light outlined by yellow light

Chapter Sixty-Six: The Plant Annwyn

x
x
x
x
o
o
o

The Plant Annwyn are said to be the watery beings of Elfin and Faerie nature. They call to mind the fact that we evolved from out of the sea. Not merely the seas and oceans of water but the sea of starlight from beyond. This oracle then speaks of our deep unconscious and calls you to examine why you want what you are asking of the oracle in the first place. What is it that calls to your deepest desires and needs in this situation? There must be something primal, something of the lizard brain that is involved in this issue. This is not necessarily a bad thing but it is something you may wish to reflect upon thoroughly.

It is possible that there are deeper issues and movements regarding this question than you previously realized. And it is quite possible that you are in some ways acting merely as a tool for others in this situation without actually realizing this is so. Once again, examine this issue thoroughly and look to its roots and deepest origins. This is usually the work of Sorcerers and if you are not a sorcerer yours'elf you may wish to find one to help you explore this situation. In the modern world, sorcerers often make a living as psychologists and dream tenders.

What is it of your deepest ancient faerie s'elf that is being aroused here? You may wish to know for it could tell you a great deal about yours'elf. In finding out what your true motives are, or the motives of others involved, much of significance can be revealed. In learning this, you may proceed with greater confidence.

Mantra:

An Eltar lythïn

Pronounced: Ane Eel – tayr lith - in

Meaning: From Nature grown

Mudra:

Have the dominant hand in mudra seven and the assisting hand in mudra one. Elbows bent at your sides, have both lower arms forward at the forty-five degree angle to the body but at a ninety degree angle to the upper arms, so the dominant hand is resting on top of the assisting hand, with palms inward forming a triangle from the body. Use the assisting hand to push the dominant hand upward toward the dominant shoulder until the dominant hand is at the shoulder, with the top of the hand toward rear and the outstretched fingers of the assisting hand pointing off and away from the body at forty-five degree angle from the shoulder.

Visualization:

Bright yellowish amber light

Chapter Sixty-Seven: The Alchemists

o
o
x
x
x
x
x

Alchemists are noted traditionally for attempting to turn base metals into gold. This is not, as some may think, an impossible ambition, it is really just a matter of adding or subtracting a few electrons from one element to create another. There is little doubt, at least these elves have none, that this will be practical science someday, and we suspect that there were indeed some alchemists of the past who knew of this and many other secrets about creating things that escape us today. The nanotechnology of creating Damascus steel is surely one of these.

This oracle then indicates that you have an opportunity to get much more out of this situation than you first realized, suspected or even strove to achieve. With the right combination of elements, of people or actions, the outcome may prove to be far more than you expected. There are hidden treasures in this situation that may be discovered if you just realize this is the case and you play your cards right, as the saying goes.

Consider well those you are involved with and how the pairing of certain individuals may produce amazing results. It might be time to introduce some of your friends to each other and to see what develops.

Mantra:

Tae cortae nao

Pronounced: tay – core – tay nay - oh

Meaning: The proper mix

Mudra:

Position the dominant hand in mudra one and the assisting hand in mudra two. Have the dominant hand and arm straight out to your side at shoulder height, palm downward. Have the assisting hand across the body at solar plexus level, also palm downward. Keeping the assisting hand in place, bring the dominant hand in so the elbow is bent outward to one's side but the hand is now over one's chest, palm downward, about four inches above the assisting hand.

Visualization:

Golden light outlined by luminous red

Chapter Sixty-Eight: The Healers

O
O
X
X
X
X
O

This is, of course, a very good sign and indicates that the situation will be improving and it urges you to apply all your energy to making things better for all concerned. This ability to heal yours'elf and others is part of your elven heritage. When we seek to make things better for ours'elves and all our others, without harming (do no harm) anyone, we put ours'elves in line with the Shining Ones and the Divine Magic whose intention is the liberation and upliftment of all beings and the all of life.

However things have been developing with the question you have asked of the oracle, we can be certain that at this point there will be improvement. If there have been difficulties, things will get better, if things have been going well, things will get even better still. Where you receive this sign in the series of seven oracles will determine when its effects will take place.

The important thing, however, is to not just stand idly by but to pitch in with this movement toward improvement. Apply your healing abilities however great or small they may seem to you and in that way increase through use, exercise and practice, those elfin healing skills. It may be that in the long run that will prove much more important than the fulfillment of your more immediate desires.

Mantra:

Ena cesdas fost

Pronounced: E – nah cess – dace foe-st

Meaning: With soothing touch

Mudra:

Begin with the dominant hand in mudra one and the assisting hand in mudra two. This movement is almost the direct opposite of the previous one. Have the assisting hand and the dominant inward across your chest, palms downward, the assisting hand at solar plexus level and the dominant hand about four inches above it. Leaving the assisting hand in place, move the dominant hand outward to its on side until it is directly out from one's shoulder.

Visualization:

Reddish golden light

Chapter Sixty-Nine: The Blue Boar

X
O
X
O
O
O
X

The boar is a symbol of might and power and the fact that this is the Blue Boar relates it particularly to the Pictish/pixie folk who painted thems'elves with woad or blue dye. The boar is usually somewhat reticent, which is to say it hides in the deep woods, but when its realm gets intruded upon it becomes extremely dangerous. Thus in receiving this oracle one is reminded to be strong but not aggressive unless endangered. Make progress on this issue but keep mainly to yours'elf unless others deliberately interfere and then you may proceed with great energy to remove that interference.

The boar is often noted for its thick hide, so don't take insults personally and don't let yours'elf be manipulated by aspersions. And while it is true that a boar has a somewhat bristly and prickly hide, you don't need to be prickly and bristly in dealing with people unless necessary. Let your bristles serve as a warning but don't get caught up in continuing personal struggles; that will only delay the fulfillment of your desires. Control your strength and your power. Respond from strategy not from passion.

This sign, however, does not necessarily mean you will encounter problems or opposition. Its main directive is to make steady progress, ignoring all that is extraneous and of no lasting significance. Protect yours'elf and your kin but keep your eyes fixed firmly upon the goal.

Mantra:

La eladur mard

Pronounced: Lah e – lay – dur may-rd

Meaning: By royal right

Mudra:

Put the dominant hand in mudra eight and the assisting hand in mudra three. Have the assisting hand bent at elbow, hand up, outstretched fingers toward ceiling/sky, palm toward rear, dominant hand palm toward body, outstretched fingers toward opposite shoulder. Bring the dominant hand down until it is out from its own side, outstretched fingers pointing downward about three feet out to your side. Simultaneously, bring the assisting hand down and across the body at chest, palm inward.

Visualization:

White light outlined by orange light

Chapter Seventy: The White Sow

x
o
x
o
o
o
o

The White Sow is a symbol of the Great Mother Goddess and she is usually attended by seven piglets, (seven being an especially sacred and meaningful number to the elves, thus our seven pointed elven star). White is usually symbol of purity, although in Buddhist literature this being is not white but of crystal diamond nature. Both of these however indicate Nature in its giving aspect. Nature nurtures all beings. A good mother loves all her children and nourishes them all. Thus in receiving this oracle remember to take care of all things involved in this question and to nurture everyone who is a part of it or who has contributed to its fulfillment.

Due to the fact that symbolically she is often shown to have seven children, we are called to consider that the fulfillment of this question may come in a number of different forms and ways. You should also reflect upon what the long terms effects of this wish may be upon fulfillment and the possibility that the result of this oracle is that you will be faced with a number of different and varied opportunities and possibly therefore a decision to make about how to proceed into the future.

This sign is surely a blessing for you. The beneficent forces of the Universe are acting in your favor and on your behalf and you can be certain that some blessings, perhaps a number of blessings, will manifest that will aid you toward your goal.

Mantra:

Konåkorla matiïn

Pronounced: Co – nah – core – lah may – tie – in

Meaning: Abundantly shared

Mudra:

Place dominant hand in mudra eight and assisting hand in mudra three. Have both hands behind your back above waist height, the dominant hand higher than the assisting hand, palms away from body. Keeping the assisting hand in place, bring the dominant hand around to the front of the body at solar plexus level, palm downward toward floor/ground and then move it a little forward and downward as though you are stroking something's head.

Visualization:

Radiant light orange glow

Chapter Seventy-One: The Basilisk

o
o
o
x
o
x
x

The Basilisk is a legendary creature, whose name means little king, and is thought to be the king of snakes and reptiles and capable of causing death with a single glance. In this way the Basilisk is related to Medusa, the snake headed being whose gaze would turn individuals into stone and also Balor the one-eyed king of the Formorians of Irish lore whose gaze would wreck destruction (rather like a laser beam, we expect). The Basilisk is sometimes said to be small snake with so much venom it leaves a snail-like trail of it.

In getting this oracle, you are called to pay attention to small and seemingly insignificant things. They may seem harmless but really they can cause you quite a bit of trouble if you are not careful. Also, because of the deadly gaze of the Basilisk, you may be wise to consider the feelings of those you encounter. There are certain lowly sorts for whom extended eye contact is perceived of as a challenge (dogs, lions and other beings are also this way), and who when they feel disrespected can be dangerous. In as much as possible it is best to keep away from these individuals if you can, but if you do encounter them, neither hold their gaze nor fearfully avoid it. A passing glance, with no expression of judgment, is enough.

There is danger in receiving this oracle, and it warns of a potential dark time and nefarious individuals. Keep a low profile and wait things out as you move cautiously upon your way. The time will change but there is little you can do to hurry its passing.

Mantra:

Ena tolk kerohaïn

Pronounced: E – nah toll-k key- row – hah – in

Meaning: With glance averted

Mudra:

Begin with the dominant hand in mudra three and the assisting hand in mudra eight. Have outstretched fingers toward ground/floor, arms crossed at elbows, dominant arm over assisting arm, palms toward rear. Now, uncross the arms and move them outward, each to its own side, pointing about three feet out, as in the signal used in some games to indicate a player has reached a base safely.

Visualization:

Neon orange light outlined by white light

Chapter Seventy-Two: The Black Dog

o
o
o
x
o
x
o

The Black Dog is a form of the Hellhound and is related to Cerberus, the hound of Hades of Greek mythology that guards the gates of Hell/Hades/the Underworld. Remember the Underworld is often seen as the realm of the Fae.

The Black Dog is usually a warning. As the hound of the Wild Hunt, it has the aspect of functioning as the stalking dog of Karma. Examine yours'elf closely to be sure that there isn't anything you are doing or have done that is interfering with the progress of your magic toward the fulfillment of the desire about which you have inquired of the oracle. If there is, act as much as possible to undo or redo what is necessary to get things flowing again. You might think of this situation as a clogged toilet. If you don't unclog it, things are just going to get worse and worse.

Since the Black Dog is often associated with death, there is a good possibility that something will be changing in this situation in a fundamental way. This may alter your outlook and your intended goal altogether. Again, clearing your path is the best way to proceed, then whatever happens will be for the best in the long run, and most importantly you won't be karmically responsible if things do go wrong.

Mantra:

Tat ris tat El me

Pronounced: Tate rice tate L me

Meaning: As fast as I may

Mudra:

Start with the dominant hand in mudra three and the assisting hand in mudra eight. Place the assisting hand so it is just on the front of your same side hip, fingers pointing downward at a forty-five degree angle. Have the dominant hand with the circle formed by the thumb and index finger against the hip, palm thus to rear. Move the dominant hand outward to the side, away from the body, make a complete loop and then move the hand forward so it is in front of the body, outstretched fingers pointing slightly downward toward floor/ground.

Visualization:

Bright orange light outlined in silver

Chapter Seventy-Three: The Bee

x
x
o
x
o
x
x

The Bee is the symbol of the elvish Merovingians who were a Frankish dynasty. The bee is a colony creature thus this is a symbol of family and of cooperation toward a common goal that benefits everyone. Therefore, this is a good omen if, in fact, you are working toward the general welfare and keeping in mind your elfin kin even if the desired outcome of your question is more individual than collective.

You may also consider how your kindred and elfin family may help you with this goal, although in doing so it is important to also examine how they may benefit by doing so. It is possible that they would help you simply out of the love and friendship that they hold for you and the goodness of their hearts but you, at the same time, would do best to make your success theirs as well. It is always good to reward those who have been of service to you.

Bees, of course, not only pollenate flowers, thus serving Nature and Life overall, but also create honey, that wondrously sweet nectar of the Divine. Serve Life in what you do and create honey in your life and you will be truly blessed by the Shining Ones and everything will turn out as you desire or quite possibly even better.

Mantra:

Grymbidas eldan

Pronounced: Grim – by – dace eel – dane

Meaning: Working together

Mudra:

Have the dominant hand in mudra three and the assisting hand in mudra five. Place the assisting hand, wrists crossed, palms downward, over the dominant hand in front of the body. Tap the assisting wrist twice upon the dominant wrist then move the dominant hand under and then over the assisting hand so it is above about three inches but not touching.

Visualization:

Luminous orange light outlined by green light

Chapter Seventy-Four: The Good Folk

x
x
o
x
o
x
o

If you obtain this sign in the series of seven you are blessed by the Good Folk, the elfin faerie folk, who are also called the good neighbors. Are you a good neighbor? That's what is important here. If you are a good neighbor, as best as you may be, then the good neighbors will do all that they can to further your efforts toward your goal, as indicated by your question, by means of effort and action upon the astral and etheric planes of being. Be a good neighbor, one of the good folk, a good family member, a good roommate, a good housemate, a good member of your community whatever it may be. Great benefits will accrue from this.

Be good to your neighbors and even if they are not the best of neighbors, be courteous and polite. This is much more important than most folks realize. Courtesy is an elven magic of tremendous power that acts very slowly and subtly but affects the deepest foundations of the human psyche. Charm, but particularly courtesy, are effective means of furthering your ambitions concerning this question. Be sure to thank the spirits for their aid and assistance and always treat them with respect. You don't have to be overly demonstrative about this. It really doesn't matter if other people notice you or not, the spirits and the Shining Ones, the Good Folk will take heed and that is what is really important, that and even more so the positive development and effect upon your own character and personality.

Mantra:

Lifla båïn

Pronounced: Life – lah bah – in

Meaning: Kindly done

Mudra:

Start with the dominant hand in mudra three and the assisting hand in mudra five. Have the assisting arm directly out to your side at shoulder height, palm to the front. Have the dominant hand, across body about six inches beneath assisting arm, palm upward. Keeping the assisting arm in place, bring the dominant arm forward and outward, as though offering something or displaying something, then continuing outward loop it around and bring it forward in a sort of stopping motion, wrist bent upward, palm now to front.

Visualization:

Bright orange light outlined by light green

Chapter Seventy-Five: The Stag

x
o
x
o
x
x
x

The Stag is a symbol of independence. He ever goes his own way no matter what others are doing or thinking. In receiving this oracle it is an indication that you may be encountering those who wish to go their own way, who see things differently, who don't agree with your opinions, ambitions or point of view concerning this issue, but that need not concern you. What is important is that you pursue your path toward your goal without getting entangled in conflict with others. You don't need to argue about things. You don't need to prove you are right. The outcome and fulfillment of your ambitions will be proof enough.

What is important is that you treat others with respect and while you don't need to agree with them, or they with you, it is vital that you acknowledge their right to believe as they choose. This is a live and let live oracle. We agree to disagree. Or as we elves say, let us all do our own thing together.

And while you may not agree about everything, particularly concerning the issue raised by the question you have put to the oracle, that doesn't preclude all possibilities of agreement. Seek common ground on some other issue or activity and let that be the bridge between you. If you do that, good fortune will arise from your efforts and you will transform possible interference to tolerance and that is a positive development.

Mantra:

La jaltli nar medli

Pronounced: Lah jail-t – lie nair mead - lie

Meaning: By leaps and bounds

Mudra:

Place the dominant hand in mudra four and the assisting hand in mudra three. Have both hands to your front, about solar plexus height, palms downward, thumbs and upper side of hands touching, outstretched fingers pointing away from the body. Move both hands forward and away from the body together, slowly but with determination.

Visualization:

Purple light outlined in orange

Chapter Seventy-Six: The Griffin

x
o
x
o
x
x
o

The Griffin is a creature whose body resembles the mixture of other creatures. It is thus a hybrid being and speaks to us therefore of mixing various aspects of our being or a variety of methods for attaining what we desire. Also consider that those who may help you with the fulfillment of this desire may not be directly related to it, which is to say, may have skills from other or related fields that may be of value to you. This is one of the reasons the character Sherlock Holmes has Dr. Watson around (besides paying half the rent). Dr. Watson is not an expert detective but he does provide insights and information that is valuable to Sherlock in his investigations.

Thus this is the place of analogy and metaphor. Look to sports, if that is your interest, or movies or books to provide some insight into this situation and how to proceed. Fairytales were designed in many ways for this very purpose. These elves use the Tarot and I Ching, therefore after consulting this oracle you may wish to look at another oracle as well for further insight and inspiration.

Also, remember the Griffin can fly. He is able to rise above the petty prejudices and obstructions that often confront those of mixed race or being, those of us who are mutants, in the normal world. You may be obstructed, but the solution here is not to confront the obstruction or obstructers directly but to rise above the situation and seek the higher ground or perhaps in some cases, the underground, the unseen realms where we become out of sight and out of mind of the normal folk.

Mantra:

Eldro onlerïn

Pronounced: Eel – drow ohn – leer - in

Meaning: Power restrained

Mudra:

Start with the dominant hand in mudra four and the assisting hand in mudra three. Begin in the position that the last one ended, which is to say with both arms out to the front, outstretched fingers pointing away from the body and palms downward toward floor/ground. Now bring both hands toward the body, separating them as you do so and turning them until they are at their respective shoulders, palms toward rear and outstretched fingers pointing toward sky/ceiling. Then immediately turn them so the palms are to the front, outstretched fingers still upward, and move them slightly forward again.

Visualization:

Vibrant violet light outlined in orange light

Chapter Seventy-Seven: The Prophet

o
x
o
x
o
o
x

The Prophet indicates foresight, the ability to gaze into the future, which is to say look at the present and determine the probable outcome of the conditions that are currently in motion according to their material and spiritual trajectory. Some individuals have an ability to tap into the Soul of the Universe, via their own souls, and in this way see the hidden movements of Life.

In receiving this sign, you are called to pause and look at the progress of events toward the fulfillment of your wish. The future is not set in stone, however, things are in motion and there is a likelihood that if things continue as they have been a particular outcome can be perceived. Is this the outcome you desire? If not, see what you can do to subtly alter the direction of events. Powerful, sudden changes are not recommended. They tend to provoke resistance and very seldom have enduring effects. Gradual change, however, is less likely to be noticed and it gives the other individuals involved a chance to adapt as the energy alters.

Remember probable is not absolute. If you can do nothing on the material plane, work on the more subtle planes of being. Do your magic and bide your time. If you receive this as the child, the final oracle, it indicates that success concerning the question you have asked will take longer than you realized or anticipated.

Mantra:

Tat larnframïn

Pronounced: Tate lair-n – frame - in

Meaning: As foretold

Mudra:

Place the dominant hand in mudra seven and the assisting hand in mudra six. Have both hands out to your sides, hands downward, palms to front. Then bring them together in front of your solar plexus area until the outstretched fingers, the index finger and the pinkie of the assisting hand, are touching the knuckles of same fingers of the dominant hand, palms toward body.

Visualization:

Amber light outlined in blue light

Chapter Seventy-Eight: The Visionary

o
x
o
x
o
o
o

Unlike the Prophet, which is the oracle before this one, the Visionary does not so much see what is likely and probable to occur but what is possible and can be achieved if you work unremittingly toward your goals. The Visionary envisions the best possible outcome for the question you have put to the oracle.

What is the very best that you can expect in terms of this issue? Not only what you desire but what would be perfect? And how do you get from here to there? Positive thinking is not an absolute. At least not for us materially bound elfin on this plane of existence. However, it is, none-the-less, a power that can be utilized to help achieve what you desire. Keep your vision in mind. Remove all doubt and focus on the best possible outcome, even if it involves a bit of fantasy. It is not that you will necessarily achieve it all, or not necessarily right away, or even in this lifetime, or on this plane of existence, but it will increase your changes of success and heighten the energy that surrounds this issue.

Don't let the fact that things may not turn out exactly as you've imagined deter you. Keep imagining. It is a magnet drawing your desires ever closer to completion.

Mantra:

Tat El tajilo

Pronounced: Tate El tay – ji - low

Meaning: As I envision

Mudra:

Start with the dominant hand in mudra seven and the assisting hand in mudra six. Place assisting hand behind your back, palm away from the body, back of hand resting on buttock, outstretched fingers pointing down at a forty-five degree angle. Have the dominant hand akimbo, which is to say fist on same side hip, palm to rear, elbow out to side. Now, keeping the dominant hand in place, bring the assisting hand out and across the body in front until its outstretched fingers rest on either side of the dominant hand's elbow.

Visualization:

Bright amber light outlined in light blue

Chapter Seventy-Nine: The Pyromage

o
o
x
o
x
o
x

The Pyromage is a magician whose power lies in mastery over fire. On the higher planes of being, material fire (if you can really call fire material) becomes light and energy. In a very real sense, movie and book wizards who project fire or beams of light from their hands or wands are pyromages, masters of energy and thus of transformation. (Note that healers also often use this energy.)

When you receive this oracle, it is a sign to put forth some energy, particularly in terms of light, to transform the situation. This is your opportunity to alter and transmute the course of things. Where you receive this oracle in the series of seven determines when your chances of success in using this energy and making a change or increasing your probability of success is greatest.

So rub your palms together. Get that static electricity going and set the energy in motion. Energize your desires and the chances are good that things will change for the better and all you hoped for will be achieved. The fulfillment of this wish is totally within your power, just be sure this is what you really desire and it is truly for your own well being, evolutionary development and the betterment of all.

Mantra:

Ena furnath fadofodur

Pronounced: E – nah fewer – nayth fay – doe – foe – dur

Meaning: With fiery determination

Mudra:

Position the dominant hand in mudra six and the assisting hand in mudra two. Have both hands down by your sides, palms toward front. Bring them both up to shoulder height, elbows bent, so that the palms are to the rear and then bringing them down again, turn the hands as you do so, so that the palms are facing to the rear as you lower them, the outstretched fingers now pointing toward the ground/floor about three feet in front of the body.

Visualization:

Luminous blue light outlined by red light

Chapter Eighty: The Necromage

o
o
x
o
x
o
o

A necromancer communicates with the dead, with the ancestors via dreams, channeling or oracles. This, however, is the sign of the necromage who utilizes the wisdom of the past, the knowledge of the dead to do magic. Most folks when they speak of necromancers are really talking about necromages, those magicians that evoke the dead as spirits to do their biding.

In getting this oracle, one is advised to consider carefully the past, to remember history as a guide for one's actions and to use the ancient wisdom to increase one's likelihood of success concerning this issue. If one receives this sign in one of the first places, particularly the first grandparent, then it is probable that this wish stems from a magic from the past, perhaps even a not yet fulfilled desire or aspiration of one of your previous lives. If you get it in the final place, the place of the child, then the chances are that someone from the past, or events of the past will greatly affect the outcome.

Whatever you do, consider what your ancestors would have done in this situation and what they desired for you. Reach into the deepest recesses of your unconscious and the collective unconscious and let your intuition guide you. Then you will find the right path and you will do the magic that leads to success. And most of all, let the spirits of your ancestors aid you. Clearly, this is their wish for you as well.

Mantra:

An elan leali

Pronounced: Ane e – lane lee – ah - lie

Meaning: From ancient days

Mudra:

Begin with the dominant hand in mudra six and the assisting hand in mudra two. Have both hands so the outstretched fingers are touching your temples. Then bring them downward so the hands come to the sides about midway, palms downward, with your elbows pointing out the back and then bring the hands straight forward and so the arms straighten out.

Visualization:

Radiant blue light outlined in light red

Chapter Eighty-One: The Boggart

x
o
o
o
x
x
x

Boggarts, alas, can be a bit miserly. They have a tendency to hoard things and in receiving this oracle, it is likely that you are dealing with individuals who just don't want to let go of whatever it is that will further you toward your goal. It is also possible and quite likely that at the point you receive this in the series of seven oracles, that things will just trickle in and you will experience very limited progress. Don't let that worry you. Make the most of the situation and what is available for you to work with and continue onward. It may be slow progress but it is progress.

Remember, the nature of misers is greed. When they perceive that they will get more from your success, they will give you a bit more. Not eagerly, of course, in fact probably quite reluctantly, but again do all you can with what you have and if you can move things along with a little, more will be forthcoming.

It is also possible that in getting this sign you will be called on to move your wish forward though various fees for permits or other things that require a bit of subtle rewarding of those who can open the way for you. They need to get their "taste" in advance, so to speak, and if you don't comply (and sometimes you may have no choice in the matter) things will just be endlessly delayed. This is not the best of situations, but it is what you are dealing with and you might as well get on with it.

Mantra:

Makli larynsol

Pronounced: Make – lie lair – ren – soul

Meaning: Fears insubstantial

Mudra:

Put the dominant hand in mudra four and the assisting hand in mudra seven. Place both hands in front of your stomach, palms toward body, the dominant hand above the assisting one by several inches. Begin winding the hands around each other about seven times, down, under, up and around, until the dominant hand comes to rest in front of the assisting hand, the assisting hand thus closer to the body.

Visualization:

Bright violet light outlined by amber light

Chapter Eighty-Two: The Hobgoblins

x
o
o
o
x
x
o

A hobgoblin is a half-goblin. Thus Tolkien's Hobbits are halflings. What we are not told is what those halves are. If a goblin is half goblin then what is the other half? Dwarf? Gnome? Thus in obtaining this oracle you are confronted by a situation in which at least half of what is going on is obscured to you. There is an iceberg, so to speak, in your path and you can only see its top and have no idea how big it may be under the surface. In such a situation, it is best to proceed slowly and carefully until you do know the extent of the obstacle you are facing.

Alas, it is quite possible that you just wish it to happen and happen now or very soon. However, rushing toward your goal or trying to force your way forward at this juncture is ill advised. First, find out what you are dealing with and then continue onward. Don't hurry into trouble.

It is also possible that you may encounter some social prejudice. Mutants and halflings, and other people of mixed race are often discriminated against by both of the races that they are combined of. Understand this as you proceed and find friends and assistance among those who are open-minded and openhearted and then you will have some success. Unfortunately, if you receive this oracle in the last place, the place of the child, it is possible that you will only get half of what you desired. Still, that's better than nothing, and you can advance from there toward a more fulfilling situation.

Mantra:

Ton fynsfofli

Pronounced: Tone fins – foe-f (rhymes with loaf) - lie

Meaning: On tiptoes

Mudra:

Have the dominant hand in mudra four and the assisting hand in mudra seven. Both arms should be directly out to the side, straight from the shoulder, palms toward the front. Bring them both inward until they cross each other, palms downward, dominant arm over assisting arm, elbows close and arms touching near elbows.

Visualization:

Luminous purple light outlined by bright amber

Chapter Eighty-Three: The Mesmerist

x
x
o
o
o
x
x

Mesmerists use the energetic power of their aura channeled and focused through their hands to touch and affect the etheric body of another, soothing or reorganizing that individual's energy. It is in a way a system of touching without physical contact. Thus in obtaining this oracle one is faced with a situation where one is called on to affect others that one cannot touch or contact directly. How do we do that? We use the power of the electro-magnetic energy of our bodies to touch others at a distance. You may wish to check out the Reiki forms for distant healing.

Use your hands, project your energy, shape the world as you wish it to be. You have the power to fulfill this wish through magic and energetic projection. Build what you want with your hands in the etheric realms and this will help it formulate upon the material planes of existence. Remember in doing the seven mudra movements that you received in response to your question that you are granting the wish that you desire. Bringing it to life with every movement of your hands.

You got this. Just keeping putting the energy toward your wish as indicated by your question of the oracle and patiently construct the outcome you envision. This is a good sign because now the power is in your hands.

Mantra:

La honsi dinkoraïn

Pronounced: Lah hone – sigh dine – co – ray – in

Meaning: By gesture activated

Mudra:

Position the dominant hand in mudra two and the assisting hand in mudra five. Have both hands, elbows at sides, lower arms straight forward from body, outstretched fingers forward, palms downward toward floor/ground. Lift both hands at the wrists so they are like a cobra's head and then strike them both downward outstretched fingers pointing toward the ground/floor.

Visualization:

Radiant red light outlined by green light

Chapter Eighty-Four: The Mystic

x
x
o
o
o
x
o

Upon receiving the Mystic you are called to open yours'elf to the intuitive realms of being, to clear your mind through meditation or some other technique and let the energy of your unconscious and thus the Universe at large speak to you and guide you. It is likely that you will receive a dream or encounter some other omen that has to do with this issue. However, don't just grab any dream. Wait for one that really speaks to you. One that you cannot ignore. It may very well come in the form of a nightmare, just to get your attention, but it will certainly seem mysterious to you and perhaps puzzle you as well. Pay close attention to what was occurring before it became a nightmare. If you are one of those who don't dream, and what elf doesn't dream, the Universe will speak to you in some other way.

It could also come in the mode of some communication, a casual encounter or some other communication that strikes you as a bit odd and most likely off the wall or out of place. Do not ignore this sign or brush it away. If it makes you wonder what it was all about; it was all about you figuring it out. There is a hint hidden here. Something that will further you on your course toward the achievement of your goal.

The important thing is to be open to the guidance of the Universe without jumping to conclusions about what it is saying or when it is speaking. If you are uncertain if it is a sign, then it's not. When it speaks you will know it. Although, what it means in saying it is another question.

Mantra:

Joul esokyn lifardurli

Pronounced: Jo – yule e – so – kin lie – fair – dur - lie

Meaning: Through arcane revelations

Mudra:

Position the dominant hand in mudra two and the assisting hand in mudra five. Have both hands, elbows bent at sides, palms upward, lower arms at a forty-five degree angle to the upper body. Move hands outward slightly and downward, turning as they do so that the palms turn toward each other and then turn back again in a scooping motion near your belly and then rise again to their previous position, turn palms downward and drop the hands, coming to a rest about four inches from their starting point.

Visualization:

Deep red light outlined by light green

Chapter Eighty-Five: The Will-o-wisp

o
x
x
x
x
x
x

The Will-o-wisp is a light in the distance, dancing around, flickering from afar, calling you to follow. Sometimes such things are mirages. You think you see something of importance but it is just an illusion leading you astray. But in this case, you may follow this distant sign, like the candle in the window of our elven home guiding you to us, with confidence. The sign may not be entirely clear. The light may, as we say, flicker, be there and then gone and then back again. But if you follow these little hints from the spirit world, you will get closer toward the fulfillment of your goal and you will surely get more signs later on.

The Will-o-wisp, as should be clear, is not a sign to be entirely depended upon. One never knows when you will see it and it could appear here only to pop up over there later on, which is to say, don't take this sign as absolute but a sort of road sign that says, go here now and then later tells you to go somewhere else, often directing you to go someplace or do something that seems utterly contradictory to what you just did or opposite to the direction you just went in. But remember, when driving down the road, you have to weave one way and then the other, back and forth, to stay in the center of the road, which itself is ever changing. The important thing here is to remain flexible and adaptable and continue to follow the signs toward success and this will bring good fortune.

Mantra:

Ver orfa tendïn

Pronounced: Veer or – fah teen-d (rhymes with fiend) - in

Meaning: In distance spied

Mudra:

Put the dominant hand in mudra one and the assisting hand in mudra four. Have both hands up, by their respective ear, elbows to the front, palms toward ear, outstretched fingers toward rear. Keeping the assisting hand in place, bring the dominant hand down so the elbow comes to the side, the hand twists in a quick flip so the outstretched fingers now point toward ceiling/sky and the palm is to the rear. Now, bring the assisting hand down and cross over the body so the palm is to body and the outstretched fingers end up resting on the forearm of the dominant hand.

Visualization:

Vibrant yellow light outlined in purple light

Chapter Eighty-Six: The Pegasus

o
x
x
x
x
x
o

The Pegasus is, of course, a winged horse, and thus represents the ability in this situation to rise above obstacles and to make rapid progress. This is surely a good sign, but you wouldn't wish to fly so high that you lose touch with the material world. After all that is most likely where the fulfillment of your wish is to be found.

On the other hand, if your question is primarily of a spiritual kind or involves relationship, then much can be gained by musing on what you may do to move things along with a little air energy, which is to say communication in its various forms. Song or poetry is also very much in order. There is even a possibility that the solution to this question will involve air travel.

You may feel at ease in obtaining this sign, but don't relax so much that you fail to continue to make effort. Rather, make hay while the sun shines, as the saying goes or as we elves sometimes say: fire the arrow when the target is in view, which is to say take advantage of your opportunities when they present themselves.

Mantra:

Luftdas usel wyl inthaïn

Pronounced: lou-ft (rhymes with roofed) – dace you – seal will ine – thah – in

Meaning: Rising above all obstacles

Mudra:

Start with the dominant hand in mudra one and the assisting hand in mudra four. Have the dominant hand across the body, palm upturned, outstretched fingers pointing toward the opposite side at about a forty-five degree angle from the body. Have the assisting hand palm downward so the outstretched fingers are on the wrist of the dominant hand as though taking one's pulse. Use the assisting hand to push the dominant hand downward, while having the dominant hand pull away from the assisting hand as though escaping from it, turning over as it does so the palm turns downward to floor/ground and the outstretched fingers flick out and move to the front.

Visualization:

Luminous golden light outlined in violet light

Chapter Eighty-Seven: The Fox

x
x
x
x
x
o
x

The Fox is the traditional symbol of the clever and the cunning. This may apply to you in this situation, that you may find some clever way to advance yours'elf, but more than likely it is an indication that you will be approached by someone who is being clever but is not making that cleverness clear. This is to say, this individual or individuals will be attempting to fool or deceive you, pretending to be other than they are, using false representation, and more than likely tempting you while appearing to be quite harmless. Thus you are cautioned to be very careful at this point and be sure that those who represent themselves as your friends are really sincere in doing so. We elves love the clever but we admire sincerity a good deal more.

Also, in proceeding you need to be sure that your own cleverness and cunning is not being used to harm the innocent and make progress for yours'elf alone at the expense of others who have done you no harm. If you use cleverness as an aspect of personality then you may proceed with confidence for your keen intelligence will surely delight those around you.

This is a good sign for connecting with others, just be certain that the connection is mutually advantageous and then all will be well and success will come to you from this interaction.

Mantra:

La jeto u car

Pronounced: Lah gee – toe you car

Meaning: By sleight of mind

Mudra:

Position the dominant hand in mudra five and the assisting hand in mudra one. Have both hands forward, elbows bent, palms toward each other, lower arms out at a ninety degree angle to the body as though brandishing a pair of six guns. Keeping the assisting hand in place, bring the dominant hand up to opposite shoulder, tapping the top of the hand where the thumb is against that shoulder and then returning it to its original position.

Visualization:

Light green light outlined in yellow

Chapter Eighty-Eight: The Succubus

x
x
x
x
x
o
o

This sign is similar to the previous one, the Fox, however, here there is definitely someone who is looking to lead you down the garden path to a dark place where they may suck the life out of you. Unfortunately, it is very likely that you will find this invitation very tempting and somehow think that you can go along with this offer and come away unharmed. Don't be foolish. Avoid this individual and save yours'elf a lot of trouble.

It is also possible that pursuing your goal at this point will simply cost you a good deal more energy and investment than you realized. There may be extra costs that you didn't account for and you may need to ask yours'elf if this is what you really desire considering how much it is going to take to achieve what you want. It is up to you but it just may not be worth all the effort.

If you receive this in the grandparents or the parents then it is quite possible that the situation will correct itself as it proceeds. However, if you get this for the child then it is quite probable that you will obtain what you desired only to discover in time that it wasn't what you really wanted after all. Realizing that, you may wish to reconsider your ambitions concerning this issue.

Mantra:

Faornla tarytïn

Pronounced: Fay – oar-n – lah tayr – rit - in

Meaning: Politely declined

Mudra:

Start with the dominant hand in mudra five and the assisting hand in mudra one. Have both hands behind your back, palms toward rear, about waist level. Now, bring both hands to the front so they are crossing, dominant wrist over assisting wrist, palms pointing to opposite sides, outstretched fingers just off center.

Visualization:

Bright green light outlined in gold

Chapter Eight-Nine: Werewolf

O
X
X
O
O
O
X

The werewolf is the proverbial wolf in sheep's clothing. Most of the time the werewolf appears to be just an ordinary person, but at certain phases of the moon this being can transform and become quite dangerous. In getting this oracle, you are reminded that appearances can be deceiving and that the way things seem to be now is not necessarily the way they will be a month from now or as the moon goes through its phases. There are hidden aspects to this situation that are not immediately clear and you are advised to wait for a while, at least a month, before making any changes or decisions. Give things time to develop and allow yours'elf a chance to see the full range of possibilities.

It is also possible that in receiving this sign that you are dealing with moody and potentially fickle individuals. If you are thinking of approaching someone for assistance, be sure you pick the right moment. And if someone says sHe will commit hirself to aiding you, be sure you can count on that commitment, otherwise this person may change hir mind with hir next mood.

There is also a possibility that you need to consider your own energy as you move forward toward this goal. You may put out a lot of energy at first, but that doesn't mean you will be able to keep up that pace as you continue onward. Gauge your own energy and know your own cycles of ebb and flow and use this knowledge to move you toward the goal you have envisioned.

Mantra:

Usco tae halon

Pronounced: You-se – co tay hay - lone

Meaning: Beneath the full moon

Mudra:

Place the dominant hand in mudra eight and the assisting hand in mudra four. Have the assisting hand, elbow bent at side, to the front at about forty-five degree angle from the waist, palm toward opposite side. Have the dominant hand, palm downward toward ground/floor, at the same angle to the body but around six or so inches above the assisting hand, outstretched fingers toward the other side. Bring the dominant hand down, tapping the top of the assisting hand twice, then turn the assisting hand so the palm comes upward toward ceiling/sky and tap it again with the dominant hand.

Visualization:

Shiny silver light outlined in purple light

Chapter Ninety: The Shapeshifter

o
x
x
o
o
o
o

The Shapeshifter is like the werewolf except this is a being who has more control over hir transformations and can take on a variety of different forms, thus we are talking about someone who can be many things to many people. This, in itself, is neither good nor bad. It is a convenient and potentially powerful ability, but it all depends upon how it is used and whether the individual is sincere in hir dealings with the great variety of different social groups sHe functions within.

So this is a caution. The overall prognosis in receiving this is really quite good. There is great potential for success concerning the issue that you raised in inquiring of this oracle, however, there is still a potential for conflict and there is a need to be careful of those who are only out for their own selves. It is surely a good thing to be able to interact with a variety of different individuals and various social groups. It gives one range and power to connect that many, perhaps most folks, do not have. But again, the most important thing is how genuine are these relationships and can they be counted upon when it really matters? Examine this situation and ask yours'elf these questions and if things look good then surely everything will turn out as you desire.

Mantra:

Loikerdas tae eln

Pronounced: Low – eye – keer – dace tay eel-n

Meaning: Reinventing the self

Mudra:

Position the dominant hand in mudra eight and the assisting hand in mudra four. Have the assisting hand down by your side, palm to side. Have the dominant hand, elbow bent, palm to rear, fingers pointing to sky/ceiling in front of its shoulder. Bring both hands together in front of the body, as though clapping, with the dominant hand over assisting hand in front of the body about waist height.

Visualization:

Bright white light outlined in violet

Chapter Ninety-One: The Silver Tree

o
o
o
x
x
o
x

Wherever you receive this in the series of seven oracles, this is a very lucky sign. It is especially lucky when it is the first grandparent and luckiest when it comes as the child. It is a sign that the spirits bless you; that there will be a sudden boost of energy for you in terms of this question; and there will be a period of quick advancement at the time where this sign appears in the seven. Know that you are blessed and that the spirit of Elfin supports you in your endeavors.

This is especially a sign of personal, spiritual and energetic success, which is to say that the situation itself will not necessarily move but that you will feel a sudden spurt of energy that will enable you to make quick progress and to apply yours'elf toward your goal with a lot of energy for a good period of time. It won't last forever, so use this burst of power and energy while you have it.

At the same time, while the situation will not alter on its own, it is none-the-less conducive toward your efforts, so you will not encounter sudden and unexpected obstacles. The way is open but it is still you who must progress upon the way.

If your question is about personal advancement, particularly spiritual advancement, then this is a truly great sign for you, for it indicates a promotion into the higher realms of power and magical development, evolutionary movement and soulful progress. Congratulations, you are being promoted.

Mantra:

Ena tylfver eldanal

Pronounced: E – nah till-f – veer eel – day - nail

Meaning: With youth eternal

Mudra:

Have the dominant hand in mudra five and the assisting hand in mudra eight. Have the assisting hand, palm downward, in front of the body at chest level. Have the dominant hand down by your side, palm to body. Keeping the assisting hand in place, bring the dominant hand upward until it is in front of and touching the pinkie of the assisting hand, palm to opposite side, outstretched fingers pointing upward to sky/ceiling.

Visualization:

Bright green light outlined in white

Chapter Ninety-Two: The Golden Tree

o
o
o
x
x
o
o

This oracle is especially a sign of material success. If your question involves money or finances or other dealings in the material world such as property and acquisition of material goods then you are surely blessed in getting this response. The Golden Tree speaks of the manifestation and establishment of Elfin on Earth and its success therein. So if your question involves the development of an elven group, vortex or the creation of a place where you may abide together then you are greatly favored in doing so.

This is a very group oriented sign and does not, in itself, speak of spiritual progress of an individual kind, but anything to do with group activity and the prosperity of one's particular clan, band, or tribe is very much favored by this oracle.

It is likely that in getting this sign that some material benefit will come to you shortly. This may only be a small object, quite possibly of gold, but this is only a sign that something greater is coming and that your financial success is favored. You may wish to use this token as a talisman to draw more success, just as restaurants often frame the first dollar that they make as a prosperity magnet.

Mantra:

Ejarla vari låka

Pronounced: E – jayr (rhymes with hair) – lah vayr – rye lah - kay

Meaning: Happily ever after

Mudra:

Place the dominant hand in mudra five and the assisting hand in mudra eight. Have the assisting hand with palm flat against your chest. Have the dominant hand just above it, palm downward to floor/ground. Bring the dominant hand forward in front of the assisting hand, making about six to seven circles and then finally moving forward until the outstretched fingers are pointing directly away from the body and the palm is toward opposite side.

Visualization:

Luminous pale green light

Chapter Ninety-Three: The Sorcerer

o
x
x
o
x
o
x

In getting the Sorcerer, one is called to seek the roots of the issue. There is quite possibly an obstruction that you will be facing and the solution lies in discovering where the problem began. This may indeed be time consuming and quite tedious work and it is likely to exhaust you and some of your resources, however, in the long run the effort will be worth it for you will clear the path ahead of you and things will move much more smoothly from then on. If you fail to put in this effort you will most likely continue to struggle bit by bit and find in the long run that avoiding the issue will cost you more time and energy than dealing with it directly.

It may be that you don't feel capable of sorting out this mess, but if that is the case, seek out the advice of those who do know how the whole situation got started and go from there. If there is no one to aid you, you may just have to do a little sorcery on your own and delve into the shamanic and psychological realms to figure it out. Somewhere deep within you is the answer, you just need to be willing to take the time and look and be open to the truth when it confronts you.

This is not a sign of good luck, but if you put in the effort then good luck can eventually arise from your efforts.

Mantra:

Tat tae lefa lam

Pronounced: Tate tay lee – fah lame

Meaning: At the very root

Mudra:

Start with the dominant hand in mudra six and the assisting hand in mudra four. Place both hands with elbows bent at sides and hands at shoulders, outstretched fingers pointing to ceiling/sky and palms to rear. Bring both hands down to about waist height and then turn them over moving them toward the centerline of the body and closer together in front of you, palms now upward, and then back again into the previous position with palms downward and hands farther apart. These moves executed in a sort of bouncing motion.

Visualization:

Bright blue light outlined in purple light

Chapter Ninety-Four: The Exorcist

o
x
x
o
x
o
o

This oracle denotes a problem, perhaps in a form of a person, that needs to be sorted out. There are some bad vibes being projected into the situation and you more than likely are feeling a bit uneasy, wondering what is exactly going on or if something bad is about to happen. There is a need to clear the atmosphere, banish the negative energy and disperse the dark clouds that seem to be hovering near on the horizon. Someone wants to rain on your parade but if you are aware of this you can avoid most of the problems that would ensue.

While this is surely not a lucky sign, removing or transforming the psychic atmosphere that is working against you will certainly be helpful and later, if the other oracles agree, good luck may come. If you receive this as one of the grandparents then it is likely that you are beginning this project or pursuing this wish despite some strong, although perhaps unstated, objections. If you receive this as the child, the outcome, then it means that even if you have succeeded and been granted your wish there are hidden problems that still need to be resolved and quite possibly you will have aroused the jealousy of others who envy your accomplishment. If you proceed with modesty in such a case and don't lord your success over others, things should turn out well in the long run and that is what is really important.

Mantra:

Nordnåïn dolen

Pronounced: Nord – nah – in doe - lean

Meaning: Purified entire

Mudra:

Begin with the dominant hand in mudra six and the assisting hand in mudra four. Have both hands about forty-five degree angle to buttocks, outstretched fingers pointing toward the ground/floor about three feet behind the body, palms upward. Bring both hands forward to the front about waist height and bring the top of the hands together so the thumbs and index fingers are alongside each other and touching and the palms are downward.

Visualization:

Luminous blue light outlined in violet light

Chapter Ninety-Five: The Naiads

o
x
o
x
x
o
x

Naiads are waters nymphs. Getting this oracle indicates feeling connections, relationship and particularly the underlying soul that unites the all of life as an essential element of your success. Understand that the Divine Magic lives in all individuals and your progress toward the fulfillment of this question has greatly to do with your inner spiritual realization of the commonality of all humanity, of all life.

At the heart of Elfin/Faerie are the two trees (Silver and Gold, the Tree of Life Eternal and the Tree of Happiness Everlasting) that are fed by the sacred pool (Love) of Elfin. All individuals need sustenance, not just food of a material sort, but food for the mind, the spirit and the soul. Without that, one may exist but isn't really living. A time will come when material food is no longer necessary and we shall live upon the pure energy of light and spirit. When that day comes we shall truly live in the radiance Elfin.

So, look to people's hearts, be aware of individual's feelings, and if you do that with a consideration for their emotional needs, you will further your progress toward the goal that you have envisioned.

Mantra:

Ena hersår fiwe

Pronounced: E – nah hear – sar (rhymes with car) fie - wee

Meaning: With evident delight

Mudra:

Begin with the dominant hand in mudra five and the assisting hand in mudra six. Place the assisting hand down by your side, palm inward toward body. Have the dominant hand up at its ear, palm toward ear. Leaving the assisting hand in place, bring the dominant hand down and across the body so it touches the opposite shoulder, palm toward shoulder and then down to its own side, palm toward body. Then once the dominant hand is settled, bring the assisting hand up and across the body until the outstretched fingers rest upon the elbow of the dominant arm, palm inward to body.

Visualization:

Vivid green light outlined by blue light

Chapter Ninety-Six: The Water Sprites

o
x
o
x
x
o
o

The water sprites are very active and effervescent beings. They tend to be extroverts rather than have the introverted personalities that naiads often display. If you receive this oracle in the series of seven, then it is likely that you will be dealing with some very extroverted individuals, particularly those who are prone to emotional effusion, involved in your progress toward this goal.

These individuals may be quite well meaning but that doesn't mean that they won't prove to be a hindrance to your success. Be courteous but firm. Otherwise, they will simply make a mess of things. They are truly the typical bull in the china shop. If you don't set some limits, they will go on and on heedless of the disaster they are creating.

At times, these individuals can be quite helpful but they need direction and guidance. If you are able to provide it, and if you can get them to listen to you and follow the hints that you provide, all will go well. On second thought, forget about hints. These individuals don't get hints. You just have to tell them outright what you need for them to do or not do.

Mantra:

Jakadas purrefråli

Pronounced: Jay – kay – dace pure –ree – frah – lie

Meaning: Casting rainbows

Mudra:

Position the dominant hand in mudra five and the assisting hand in mudra six. Have both hands up at shoulders, elbows bent at sides, palms toward front. Bring both hands forward and down, turning as they do so in a scooping motion that brings them closer together at your waist and then back up again, so the palms are upward as the hands come up and the outstretched fingers come by and are pointing toward one's cheeks. All of this as though one is standing over a pot of steaming soup and wanting to waft the aroma to one's nostrils. End with the hands pointing out to their own sides as much as possible. The palms will probably be pointing at about a forty-five degree angle to their same side shoulders.

Visualization:

Neon green light outlined by blue light

Chapter Ninety-Seven:
The Shaman

o
x
x
x
o
x
x

The shaman indicates your power to shape what you want by doing magic on the astral and imaginal planes of being. Visualize what you desire and do what you need to do to move things along in the realms of imagination. This is particularly true when you are obstructed or things are moving slowly but there is absolutely nothing you can do of a material sort to get things unstuck; you have come to the place where WD40 just won't work. There is no action you can take, no communication you can make, nothing left to do but magic in the formative realms of the astral and imaginal worlds.

You may feel frustrated. You may feel that nothing is moving or working out the way you desire, that the fulfillment of your goal is so far in the future that you may as well give up. But don't. The Solution is to be found Elsewhere, literally. Step into Elfin. Step into the realms that are closer to the Divine Magic where one's wishes come true much more quickly than they tend to do in the slow progressing mundane and material realms, and affect things there.

Most importantly, use this magic to shift your own feelings and vision toward the realization of your desire. In those realms, especially, positive thinking is vital. See only the possibility of success. Imagine the answer to your question being the best it can be and in this case, if the last oracle, the child, doesn't suit you, do the oracle again after you have visited and done your magic on the astral planes and see what shift has occurred.

Mantra:

Pasa mistråïn uqåli

Pronounced: Pay – sah my – strah – in you – qwah - lie

Meaning: Along tangled streams

Mudra:

Begin with the dominant hand in mudra three and the assisting hand in mudra four. Have the dominant hand against its side, about solar plexus high, pinkie to side, palm upward to ceiling/sky, outstretched fingers to front, elbow protruding to rear. Have the assisting hand all the way forward, palm downward to ground/floor, outstretched fingers toward front. Now, change their positions sharply, so the assisting hand turns, comes to its own side, palm upward, elbow protruding and the dominant hand goes forward, palm turning down, outstretched fingers directly forward. Make this whole motion rather like a karate move.

Visualization:

Bright orange light outlined in purple light

Chapter Ninety-Eight: The Hedgewitch

O
X
X
X
O
X
O

There is an aspect of the impromptu, the improvisational, the ad hoc, and the make do with what you have, when getting this oracle. You may have to jerry-rig something to keep things going. You may have to fly by the seat of your pants or move forward in ways that are not traditional, that will not necessarily work but are worth trying since you can't think of anything else to do.

A change is needed in this situation. It is clear that something has to be done. But the question is what? What will really change the situation for the better and get things moving toward the fulfillment of your goals. Don't just act impulsively. Think things through. As we said, it may be that you will have to experiment and it may be unclear how things will turn out, however, don't do things for the sake of mere action. Really endeavor to fix the problem. You may not be absolutely certain of what will work; you may not have everything you need to make it work perfectly; but certainly you have some ideas of what may work and you can proceed from there as best you may. And if you don't succeed the first time …

Mantra:

Tat ter jostålu

Pronounced: Tate tear (rhymes with near) joe-ss – tah - lou

Meaning: As it happens

Mudra:

Start with the dominant hand in mudra three and the assisting hand in mudra four. Have both hands back by your ribs, thumbs against ribs, palms therefore downward to floor/ground. Now bring them both forward in a waving motion like dolphins swimming, until they reach full extension, outstretched fingers pointing forward.

Visualization:

Radiant orange light outlined by purple light

Chapter Ninety-Nine: The Magician

x
o
x
x
x
o
x

Getting this oracle is surely a good sign for it indicates your power to take action, do your magic, get things going and achieve success regarding the question you have put to the oracle. Wherever you find this particular oracle in the series of seven is very good for you. In the first place or as one of the other grandparents it indicates using magic to set things in motion at the very beginning or as you are just getting started. As a parent, it indicates using your magic to move things along and when you receive it as the child, the outcome, it not only indicates a fulfillment of your wish but also an indication that more magic and greater possibilities await you, that the success of this goal will lead you to even greater things.

So do your magic and let the energy unfold. Particularly when you get this sign you may wish to set up a time for doing the mantra and mudra series attached to the seven oracles you received in response to this inquiry on a fairly regular basis. Let it become a ritual for you, a ritual of success, abundance and prosperity. And use that success and abundance to do even greater things for yours'elf and your kindred, for that is the true magic.

Mantra:

Kalfeldås va el'na yon

Pronounced: Kale – feel – dace vah eel – nah yone

Meaning: According to my will

Mudra:

Place the dominant hand in mudra five and the assisting hand in mudra three. Have the assisting hand in front of your mouth, palm to front, which means thumb downward and pinkie up. Have the dominant hand directly in front of the assisting hand so the palm is to the opposite side, the outstretched fingers upward toward ceiling/sky, and you are able to look through the loop created by the thumb and ring finger with the opposite side eye. Now move the dominant hand directly forward about six inches.

Visualization:

Vivid green light outlined by orange light

Chapter One Hundred: The Magus

x
o
x
x
x
o
o

On receiving this oracle you are blessed and that blessing is intended to be spread outward to all the others with whom you come in contact. The Magus is a master magician. The Magus is responsible for helping to nurture the world and hir people. The Magus truly has gone beyond hir own s'elf and knows that hir people's success is hir own success as well. The Magus, in a sense, rules the world, or hir own realm, annunciates hir Vision, and sets the world in motion, but all this sHe does for the benefit of those for whom sHe has assumed responsibility. Hir life is no longer hir own, but that does not matter for sHe lives forever in hir people and all that she does is in service to those kindred.

This oracle is a sign of advancement. Your magic is being heightened, your powers will be increased, but so will the responsibilities that you bear. In many ways, it no longer matters if your wish or question to the oracle is fulfilled. What matters is that you use whatever success you have for improving the lives of all those around you. Congratulations, you have become a magical parent.

Mantra:

Fro tae elyn u wyl

Pronounced: Fro – tay e – lynn you will

Meaning: For the benefit of all

Mudra:

Position the dominant hand in mudra five and the assisting hand in mudra three. Have the assisting hand in front of you, palm downward, forearm about six to eight inches from chest, outstretched fingers pointing toward opposite direction. Have the dominant hand, palm upward, behind your back about waist height, about six to eight inches from back. Now, switch the positions of the two hands in a forceful fashion.

Visualization:

Brilliant green light outlined by pale orange light

Chapter One Hundred One: The Conjuror

O
O
X
O
O
X
X

Are you ready to conjure up some magic? To get things going the way you desire? With this oracle the time is right to use your spells and conjurations to move things further along.

Look to the place that this oracle appears in the seven and note that time, for when it occurs you will be called to conjure up something special. If it appears in the grandparents, it will probably be fairly soon, if in the parents, wait a bit but as things progress the time will come, and it could be quite suddenly so be prepared. However, if it is in the child then it is an indication that you should act just as things seem to be coming to fruition, to give them an extra boost for completion.

The significance of this sign is that there is something you can do to achieve your goals. You are not merely required to have faith and let things play out as they will, you can take action and the chances of success will be increased thereby. And while there is a possibility that you may conjure a spirit or spirits to help you with this goal, remember you are the director of their activity and need to remain active in the magic, guiding their movements. Don't micro-manage, but don't be totally hands off either.

Act with surety and confidence, with power and great energy and let your will unfold unto the world.

Mantra:

La mol kordïn masa

Pronounced: Lah mole cord – in may – sah

Meaning: By word made flesh

Mudra:

Have both hands assume mudra two. Have the palms toward each other in front of your chin, outstretched fingertips touching in a steeple effect. Then bring both hands downward, so palms are toward floor/ground and the outstretched fingertips are still touching but are now pointing directly to each other and the elbows have come upward so the forearms are straight out from the hands. Then move both hands forward and outward from the body so the outstretched fingers are pointed directly away from you and your index fingers are alongside of each other and touching.

Visualization:

Brilliant red light

Chapter One Hundred Two: The Ceremonialist

o
o
x
o
o
x
o

Ceremonial magic is formal magic. It is the magic of stability, of establishing something and carrying it on. The first artistic creation of something is often wondrous and amazing, but the job of carrying on a tradition and keeping it alive is fraught with responsibility and is no easy task. In fact, keeping things going, carrying on tradition without it becoming boring and meaningless is in many ways far more difficult than creating something amazing in the first place.

This is a challenge for you. How do you move toward your goal as indicated by the question you have put to the oracle without becoming exhausted, without giving up hope as it takes its own time toward completion, and without coming to the point where you no longer even care if it comes about or not, overwhelmed by a sense of hopelessness? And how do you continue to nurture your progress toward the fulfillment of your desires without overdoing the magic, using too much force or interfering with the spirits who are striving to fulfill your will?

A ceremony is called for, a ceremony to recognize the beginning of your magic, a ceremony to honor those who endeavor to complete it, a ceremony to celebrate its completion. What's important is that you truly feel the spirit, invest your energy into the ceremony, the magic, because if it is merely by rote you have lost touch with what is truly vital to its success.

Mantra:

Kalfeldas vah tae lyr

Pronounced: Kale – feel – dace vah tay ler (rhymes with her)

Meaning: According to the book

Mudra:

Position both hands in mudra two. Have the assisting hand behind your back at the waist, palm away from body. Have the dominant hand at a forty-five degree angle from and to the opposite side of your face, palm toward rear. Keeping the assisting hand in place, bring the dominant hand across your face and then straight out to the side from the shoulder, arm at full extension, palm downward, and then move that hand back across the body until it is against the opposite shoulder with outstretched fingers pointing toward the place where the shoulder meets the upper arm.

Visualization:

Bright light red light

Chapter One Hundred Three: The Troll

x
o
o
x
o
o
x

Trolls are generally related to the mountains and to rocks and they tend to be large, cumbersome and slow moving (although there are smaller trolls who may be more nimble), thus in attaining this oracle one is faced with the fact that at the point you receive this one among the seven oracles that things just won't be moving hardly at all and if they are progressing it will be very slowly and if you try to get things going again by interfering you will just slow things down even further, rather like speeding to get somewhere and having an accident due to your haste and then being stuck.

Don't try to push things at this point. All that is required is that you maintain progress as best you can. Keep it going, even at its slowest pace, but keep it going. Trying to move it faster at this juncture is working against the energy of the time and is a waste of your efforts. If you can keep it from going backward you are accomplishing something really great.

Later, if the other oracles agree things will pick up again and you can make more rapid progress. However, if you receive this oracle as the child, the outcome of the seven, then it is likely to take a long time to completion. On the other hand, if you do get it in that position it is also likely to endure for a long time once it does come to fruition.

Mantra:

Ena torni parser

Pronounced: E – nah tour – nigh pair - sear

Meaning: With grand flourish

Mudra:

Place both hands in mudra seven. Have both arms out to your sides at shoulder height, palms downward. Now, bring them both together in front of your face, palms toward face, forearms together and touching, fists upward, bottom of hands together, as though you are creating a shield in front of your face.

Visualization:

Luminous amber light

Chapter One Hundred Four: The Giant

x
o
o
x
o
o
o

Giants are, of course, huge. When you draw this oracle you will have to deal with someone or something of huge importance, perhaps someone in authority, or maybe simply someone who has a lot of influence in your social circle, or power over your life. At any rate, they will greatly influence this situation and there is little you can do about it except wait. This can, of course, be quite frustrating but waiting, being patient, and mostly letting their interest wander elsewhere is the best thing you can do under the circumstances. Eventually, they will get out of your way and then you can proceed.

In the meantime, it is best just to learn some patience. If you know how to meditate then this is a good time to do it, if not, it is a good time to learn. The important thing is to retreat into seclusion for the time being. Don't draw attention to yours'elf and do let things develop on their own for a while. Elsewhere, in the unseen realms there are things going on, magic moving, spirits working on your behalf. Have faith and the times will change.

If you get this as the last of the seven oracles, then, alas, you will have to wait for fulfillment. Just when it seems it is about to come true, there's a snag. But wait and completion will come, just not as quickly as you first thought.

Mantra:

Ena jolvath volth

Pronounced: E – nah joel – vayth vole-th

Meaning: With mighty roar

Mudra:

Put both hands in mudra seven. Have both hands down by sides, palms toward body. Bring them up and together at chest level so the forearms are straight out from the hands whose knuckles are pressed together. Then leaving the assisting hand in place, move the dominant hand to its side so the elbow is bent and at your side and the hand is upward, knuckles toward ceiling/sky, palm to rear. This done in a forceful manner as though it were a martial art movement.

Visualization:

Radiant amber light outlined by light amber

Chapter One Hundred-Five: The Faery Ball

x
x
o
x
o
o
x

This is a sign of progress. The Faery Ball is a gathering of diverse fae folk and thus getting this sign denotes a coming together of energy and movement toward the attainment of your goal. This, however, is not necessarily a sign of rapid progress. Alas, the elves, pixies, and fae folk of various sorts tend to arrive at the ball at different times. Faeries often like to be fashionably late. Pixies will come and go and come back again. Elves often arrive early to help set up and stay late to assist with the clean up. So the indication here is of a series of events that move you toward the fulfillment of your question. These may be quite small developments in and of themselves, but together they will push the situation forward dramatically through the course of time.

The important thing for you is to persevere. The fact that the progress is slow may lead to you believe that nothing is happening at all, but that is not the case. The steps forward may be small, but they are constantly and continuously progressive. So hang on, and keep trudging toward the goal. You are making progress even if things appear otherwise. Don't be deceived by slow progress and give up, you are reaching your goal. As long as you continue on, you will surely succeed.

Since the Faery Ball is a gathering of individuals, you may also consider who among your diverse circle of friends and acquaintances may help you with this magic. It is not wise to ask anything big from them, but little magics will all accumulate and that is what we desire after all.

Mantra:

Ver vynsae ond

Pronounced: Veer vin – say oh-nd (rhymes with phoned)

Meaning: In circle round

Mudra:

Start with the dominant hand in mudra seven and the assisting hand in mudra five. Have the assisting hand with elbow bent at side and hand up, outstretched fingers toward ceiling/sky, palm to back and the dominant hand across your body so the palm is downward and the knuckles of the hand are against the elbow of the assisting hand. Now, keeping the dominant hand in place, move the assisting hand down and forward so the outstretched fingers point away from you to the front and the palm is downward.

Visualization:

Vibrant amber light outlined by green light

Chapter One Hundred-Six: The Faerie Rade

x
x
o
x
o
o
o

Unlike the Faery Ball, which is a gathering of fae somewhere in the depths of Elfin/Faerie, the Faerie Rade is a peregrination through the world. It is a sort of touring holiday, an easy and casual expedition into the heart of the world to observe what is going on as well as to set an example and serve as an inspiration to others, nurturing and rewarding them as best you may. The indication here is therefore to go forth and nurture those you encounter, particularly among your kindred and this will in time lead to success.

It is unlikely that this action, this magic of seeding the world, so to speak, will have instant results; however, this is really about leaving breadcrumbs in the world for others to find in the course of their own explorations and evolutionary development. The important thing here is not to concentrate on the success of the question you have put to the oracles, but to instill energy into the world that will in time come back to you. Our magic always returns to us in time.

So, take your time. Relax and enjoy this process. Don't hurry toward your goal but amble toward it with an easy grace as though utterly certain and confident of your eventual success. For you will indeed succeed in time. But here, it is not the completion of the goal that is important but learning to enjoy the journey.

Mantra:

Pånddas na tosåtan

Pronounced: Pond – dace nah toe – sah – tane

Meaning: Setting an example

Mudra:

Position the dominant hand in mudra seven and the assisting hand in mudra five. Have the dominant hand across the body about waist height, palm downward, thumb and upper hand against body. Have the assisting hand elbow bent and resting on the bottom of the dominant hand, back of hand against opposite cheek, outstretched fingers pointing toward, perhaps even touching, opposite ear, palm outward away from body. Bring the assisting hand downward across body with arm at full extension, so the outstretched fingers sweep toward floor and then move out until the fingers are pointing about three feet from one's side, palm toward body.

Visualization:

Vivid amber light outlined by light green

Chapter One Hundred-Seven: The Soul Mate

o
o
x
o
x
x
x

The Soul Mate is a particularly good sign if the question you asked of the oracles concerned relationship because it indicates that the right person or persons that can bring happiness and soulful fulfillment into your life will appear or some link to them will manifest in your life at the point at which this sign designates in the series of seven. If your question concerned financial matters, then the indication is that you will meet someone who will give you inside information or some significant hint that will help your business prospects greatly. If your question centered on spiritual matters, then it is likely that you will encounter a person that will enlighten you or guide you in the direction that is most productive for your evolutionary development.

But what is certain in receiving this oracle is that someone will appear and that person's influence upon your life, if you are open to it, may be profound and bring about huge changes in the long term if not immediately so. If you are open to this influence, it will be greatly to your benefit, so treat every person you encounter as though you are meeting an elven king or queen who is going about the world in secret and in disguise and if you do that then when the right person arrives great blessings will come to you.

And if you are looking for your soul mate then sHe is likely to come into your life, or if not hir in person then someone who will eventually lead you to hir. Be of good cheer, for you are surely blest.

Mantra:

Tat vari lawaïn va te

Pronounced: Tate vay – rye lay – way – in vah tea

Meaning: As ever destined to be

Mudra:

Place the dominant hand in mudra four and the assisting hand in mudra two. Have both hands crossed at the wrists, dominant hand over assisting hand, palms to body about belly height, outstretched fingers pointing downward and off to opposite sides. Then bring both hands upward, keeping the wrists together until the wrists are touching your forehead and the palms are facing front.

Visualization:

Luminous purple light outlined by red light

Chapter One Hundred Eight: The Star Mate

o
o
x
o
x
x
o

Star Mates are different from Soul Mates. Soul Mates indicate individuals who are attached to you personally, who love you as an individual and will most likely be with you through the lifetimes, appearing again and again in your life and eventually will be with you through eternity. Star Mates, on the other hand, are associated with you due to the mission you are upon as an Elfin Being. They are part of your destiny but only in so far as you have something to accomplish together. It is not that they cannot mean more to you or you to them, but that more personal connection is not the central aspect of your relationship. This is a relationship of duty, of responsibility, of the connection to those who have sworn to enact a Vision together and who have come into a particular life in order to do so.

If you receive this sign, no matter what your question concerned, it means that the influence of your destiny and particularly the need to fulfill the oaths that you took upon the Sacred Silver Flame of Elfin will have a bearing on this issue and its outcome. Certainly, someone will appear who reminds you of this in some way and it is quite possible that you will not be able to achieve what you wish in terms of your question to the oracles until you have taken care of this bit of duty whose obligation you have voluntarily undertaken.

At the same time, you should know that in carrying out the task that is set before you by your Star Mate that you will receive the energy and magic needed to achieve your more personal goal. If it should happen that your question was about your destiny, your path or your Vision then you can count yours'elf as being especially lucky and blest in getting this response as well as getting your next assignment.

Mantra:

Ason hathïn

Pronounced: A – sone hay-th – in

Meaning: Purpose driven

Mudra:

Begin with the dominant hand in mudra four and the assisting hand in mudra two. Have both hands behind your back at waist level, assisting hand with back of hand to body, outstretched fingers toward opposite side and dominant hand with palm of the hand inward, so its outstretched fingers are touching the fingertips of the assisting hand. Leaving the assisting hand in place, bring the dominant hand around the body, touching the chest with palm downward and then move that hand straight downward with outstretched fingers pointing toward floor/ground and palm inward toward body.

Visualization:

Bright violet light outlined by red light

Chapter One Hundred Nine: The Bull

o
o
x
x
o
x
x

The Bull is a sign of strength and prosperity. If your question to the oracles has to do with financial matters this is a very good sign, particularly for investment or starting a business or enterprise. It is generally a sign that one may go for it and will meet with positive response and success. Where you receive this sign in the series of oracles will, of course, determine the period when it is best and most conducive to take action with strength and great energy. If it is one of the grandparents, then you will surely begin with tremendous power. If it is a parent, a need for more effort toward your goal will develop within about six months or so, depending on the overall period the fulfillment of your wish is likely to take. And if it comes as the child or outcome, then a burst of activity will most likely be needed, and certainly helpful, as you near completion.

So the message from this oracle says push onward. The Force is with you on this one and you may feel certain that your efforts will meet with response. But remember, such energetic movements cannot last forever. At some point you will get exhausted if you continue without a break and in time the cycles will change and the time will become less conducive to success, so take advantage of this opportunity while the time is favorable.

Mantra:

Joul ical manod

Pronounced: Jo – yule eye – cal may – node

Meaning: Through focused intent

Mudra:

Place the dominant hand in mudra three and the assisting hand in mudra two. Have both hands straight out from respective shoulders at shoulder height, palms downward, outstretched fingers pointing away from the body. Bring both hands in and cross them over your chest, dominant hand uppermost and then move them out and downward to their respective sides with palms to the front, arms about forty-five degree angle to body, outstretched fingers pointing about four feet in front and to side of body, like a painting of Jesus displaying the wounds on his hands.

Visualization:

Radiant reddish orange light

Chapter One Hundred Ten: The Cow

o
o
x
x
o
x
o

The Cow is a symbol of giving and generally of docility. When you receive this sign in the series of seven oracles it means that you should nurture this project and others involved with it in small but regular ways, which is to say it is not about giving them a lot but of continual encouragement and rewards. This is also a sign that you, yours'elf, will be receiving rewards and that in doing so it is wise to share what you get with your others.

While the Cow doesn't have the forceful energy of the Bull, it is an oracle of prosperity and success. In some ways, it is a sign of culture and civilization for it denotes stability in one's situation. Thus here we are talking about slow but sure progress that can be furthered even more through intelligent investment. As we say the results of this are unlikely to be dramatic, but they are fairly certain and you can proceed with confidence toward the realization of your goal. Just, don't rush it at this point.

And, let yours'elf be guided. If not by someone who is wise or knowledgeable that you respect and knows the way, be guided by your own intuition and inner being. This is not to say by your random or desire based thoughts but by an openness that allows you to just wander around and somehow by doing so find the right way.

Mantra:

La peddas zelsåla

Pronounced: Lah peed – dace zeal – sah – lah

Meaning: By yielding consciously

Mudra:

Start with the dominant hand in mudra three and the assisting hand in mudra two. Have the assisting hand across your body about waist height, palm to body, outstretched fingers pointing downward to opposite hip. Have the dominant hand down to its side, outstretched fingers pointing to floor/ground, palm to body. Bring the dominant hand up and touch opposite shoulder, palm to shoulder, then back down to your side, but as it passes the assisting hand, bring that hand up and to its own shoulder, palm to rear.

Visualization:

Brilliant orange light outlined by bright red

Chapter One Hundred Eleven: The Druid

x
o
x
x
o
o
x

This is a sign of knowledge and wisdom, particularly of secret knowledge, esoteric wisdom or even technical knowledge, knowledge that only those who are trained in a particular art or science are privy to. It may mean that you need to seek out someone who has the knowledge that you desire, that will aid you toward the completion of your goal as indicated by your question put to the oracles, but it is even more likely that you are called to develop your own knowledge and wisdom. That, in fact, you cannot proceed further toward your goal without discovering certain things. You need information to continue forward.

Since the Druid is also a magician or wizard of various sorts there is some indication that a bit of magic may be of help here. The type of magic depends greatly upon your own disposition and inclinations as an individual. Remember, Druids could be Musicians, Poets, Herbalists, Masters of Oracles, and have numerous other talents and are essentially researchers into and custodians of all sorts of arcane, as well as, exoteric knowledge. They knew the wisdom of the Trees and the plants, of the stars and the cycles of the Earth. So, what is your magical expertise, your field of study? And how do you deepen and enhance what you already know? While there may not seem to be a direct corollary between that study and your question, we assure you that pursuing this deeper knowledge will reveal to you something of significance relative to your ambition.

Mantra:

Ver tae dasa u tae åltitaru

Pronounced: Veer tay day – sah you tae ahl (sounds a bit like all with more of an 'ah' sound) – tie – tay - rue

Meaning: In the shade of the woodland

Mudra:

Have the dominant hand in mudra seven and the assisting hand in mudra three. Position both hands across chest, crossed at wrists, elbows bent at sides, hands toward opposite shoulders, palms inward to body then bring both hands down and forward until the palms are upward to ceiling/sky and the forearms are at a ninety degree angle to body.

Visualization:

Bright amber light outlined by brilliant orange

Chapter One Hundred Twelve: The Bard

x
o
x
x
o
o
o

The Bard is a class of Druid whose expertise lays primarily in the composition of music, poetry and thus writing, as well as, public speaking. Saruman's ability, in the Lord of the Rings books, to use the power of the Voice, like that of the Bene Gesserit in the Dune books, is an extension and development of the powers of the Bard. Thus in getting this oracle it is quite possible that you will need to express your goal and your desire to achieve this goal in some form, through music, public speaking or some other mode of communication in order to move the energy along toward fulfillment.

Remember that no matter how powerful your ability to communicate that not everyone will be influenced by what you say or write. However, that doesn't really matter. What matters is finding your audience. Finding those who are open to what you have to express and moving them with your words, your song. On all others, you are just wasting your sacred magical breath.

We know, having taught public speaking, that some folks are terrified of public performance in any fashion and so this may be a challenge for you. But remember again that the mode of communication is up to you. It could be writing or song composition. And remember also this will further the realization of your goal. So, if you are one of those who is terrified of public performance, you need to ask yours'elf how much does giving in to that fear matter in balance with how much you desire the attainment of this goal?

Mantra:

Ensåtuvarla soraïn

Pronounced: Een – sah – two – vayr – lah soar – ray - in

Meaning: Poetically conjured

Mudra:

Place the dominant hand in mudra seven and the assisting hand in mudra three. Have both hands behind your back beneath waist, palms away from body. Bring them both around to the front and place them in front of your groin area, the assisting hand over the dominant hand, as though you suddenly discovered you are naked and are modestly trying to cover up your genitals.

Visualization:

Deep amber light outlined by light orange

Chapter One Hundred Thirteen: The Raven

x
x
o
x
x
o
x

The Raven brings news, omens and signs from the world of the spirits, particularly the ancestors, therefore in getting this oracle among the seven be aware that a sign will come to you, perhaps in the form of a dream but most likely from some aspect of nature, or perhaps even in the form of an actual raven. In fact, if you have an encounter with ravens around the time this sign appears in the series of oracles, pay close attention. And if it happens that you live somewhere away from nature, pay close attention to dreams in which animals appear to you.

However, don't expect that this sign will be dramatic in presentation. It is most likely to be quite subtle and require an intuitive interpretation from you in the same way the divination devices such as the Tarot or I Ching require interpretation. Search inside yours'elf for the answer.

What this sign will mean for you, we do not know. There is no real way of knowing until you receive it. But if you are open and you follow the hints it offers you, you will find real guidance upon your path toward the realization of this goal. And while its indications may also be quite subtle, guiding you to do but little things that will have small effects, this is still progress and keeping this in mind as you proceed will prove beneficial to you.

Mantra:

Tae elan'na jålf

Pronounced: Tay e – lane – nah jahl-f

Meaning: The ancient's voice

Mudra:

Position both hands in mudra five. Have the dominant hand across your chest with palm to front, outstretched fingers pointing to opposite side and away from you. Have the assisting hand, elbow bent, palm to front, outstretched fingers pointing to sky/ceiling, and in front of and across the dominant hand, so they form a sort of 't' shape, with dominant wrist behind and touching the assisting wrist. Now, move both hands and arms so they change position, however, with the dominant wrist still behind the assisting wrist, but on its own side with outstretched fingers now toward sky/ceiling.

Visualization:

Luminous deep green

Chapter One Hundred Fourteen: The Crow

x
x
o
x
x
o
o

On receiving the Crow, you are cautioned against bragging about what it is you wish or desire in terms of this question or over-sharing with others about what your goals are and what you are doing to achieve them. In most cases communicating about your goals is a good idea, but in getting this sign it means to keep mum about what is going on, what you intend and your current endeavors.

There are times when it is best to keep a low profile. This is one of them. This is not a sign of obstruction, but of avoiding potential obstructions. It is an indication of progress but of quiet and slow progress unobtrusively carried out. If you can keep from arousing the undue attention of others, you can proceed without interference.

If your question concerned relationship, then a certain amount of humility and modesty is advised, as well as a slow, almost reluctant approach. Be ever ready to retreat at the first sign of resistance and only advance when the individual advances toward you.

Mantra:

Serytïn bronla

Pronounced: Sear – rit – in brone - lah

Meaning: Declared widely

Mudra:

Begin with both hands in mudra five. Have both hands crossed in front of your belly, palms to body, outstretched fingers pointing to ground/floor, dominant wrist over assisting wrist. Now, raise the hands together, upward, like a bird flying away from you, until you reach full arm extension and the outstretched fingers are pointing relatively upward at a forty-five degree angle from your body.

Visualization:

Vivid light green

Chapter One Hundred Fifteen: The Selkie

O
X
X
O
X
X
X

The Selkie is a being of water and land, able to live in both worlds, but generally preferring the former to the latter, and most of all, wanting the option, the choice to do as sHe pleases, to live as and where sHe wishes. In getting this oracle, it is a sign that you will be dealing with someone who is both independent as an individual and desires to retain that independence and quite possibly you may encounter someone who is very feeling oriented, most likely sensitive and highly intuitive, and who spends at least as much time in hir feelings as sHe does in the normal world of reality. Sensitivity in response to such a being is greatly advised.

There is also an indication here that a merely practical approach to this issue is not enough. You are particularly called to consider people's feelings about what is going on and what their feelings will be when you succeed. Even if, or especially if, those feelings are totally illogical.

Also, you need to consider your own energy in this situation. Don't wear yours'elf out trying to force the fulfillment of your desires with pure emotional willpower. Be practical and take things a step at a time, gauging your own energy to keep it functioning at optimal levels.

Mantra:

Lorver eltar

Pronounced: Lore – veer eel - tayr

Meaning: Second nature

Mudra:

Put both hands in mudra four. Have them up and crossed behind your head, with assisting wrist in front of dominant wrist, as though the hands form a sort of headdress. Now, bring both hands forward, uncrossing them as you do so, so that the arms come to full extension, the outstretched fingers point up and away from the body and are at about a forty-five degree angle from the body, like you are using both hands to point to some high mountain in the distance.

Visualization:

Brilliant purple light

Chapter One Hundred Sixteen: The Mermaid

O
X
X
O
X
X
O

The Mermaid is a creature of the sea. Unlike the Selkie, the Mermaids cannot shed their skin and live on land but they are half-human, of this world but not invested in it entirely. Mermaids indicate individuals who not only are very feeling oriented, perhaps very emotional, but likely love the water, love the sea, love the feeling of the surf, the ocean breeze, and the ocean spray. Surfer dudes are a prime example of this sort of individual.

In getting this oracle, you are advised to chill out a little while. Cease your efforts to attain your goal and go spend some time in Nature. Unrelenting activity and pressure will only get you so far. So, take a break, relax, go to the beach if you can, or, if not, lay in a swimming pool, a hot tub or even a bathtub and give yours'elf an opportunity to revive.

Of course, you don't want to overdo it. You do wish to get back to your efforts to achieve this goal but only after you are thoroughly refreshed. If you can do that, if you can learn to balance work and play, then this is a very good sign for you.

Mantra:

Shevurïn ver selfdas

Pronounced: She – viewer – in veer seal-f - dace

Meaning: Immersed in feeling

Mudra:

Start with both hands in mudra four. Place both hands so the elbows are bent but slightly away from the body and the outstretched fingers are pointing at an angle upward toward their same side eye, palms downward. Then, move the hands forward and away from the eyes so the outstretched fingers are pointing toward the front. This reminiscent of the motion people use with their fingers to signal they are watching someone, only with both hands.

Visualization:

Radiant violet light

Chapter One Hundred Seventeen: The Salmon

x
x
o
o
x
o
x

The Salmon is a Druidic sign of wisdom. Not intellectual and mental wisdom as the Owl tends to represent but the wisdom of feeling, relationship and experience. This is an oracle of beneficence. It is a sign of good luck and good fortune coming to you primarily because you have learned something, not intellectual knowledge, not information per se, but learned something within and about yours'elf that will affect the course of your evolution and the fulfillment of the inquiry put to the oracles.

If you receive this sign as one of the grandparents, then it is likely that you have already learned the lesson of the Salmon and will use it to initiate this project. If you receive it as one of the parents then it is likely this is an experience, transformation, and inner knowledge and knowing that will occur as things move toward your goal. If you receive it as the child, the outcome, then this wisdom will come along with the fulfillment of your question, as an added result of this quest.

What is important here is that it is more than likely that the transformation you undergo and the inner wisdom you will have obtained will prove a great deal more important in the long run than the actual realization of your wish. And even if it should happen that the wish itself isn't fulfilled the evolution of your being will make that immaterial.

Mantra:

An tae syranïn

Pronounced: Ane tay sir – rain - in

Meaning: From the enchanted waters

Mudra:

Place the dominant hand in mudra six and the assisting hand in mudra five. Have both hands up and to the dominant side cheek, with the palms toward each other, the thumbs and bent fingers touching, the outstretched fingertips touching, so the index finger of the dominant hand is against the index and middle fingers of the assisting hand, and the pinkies are touching, the outstretching fingers are pointing to the sky/ceiling, and the bottom of the hands are to the front. Now bring both hands down together in a scooping motion in front of the body and then up to the same position on the opposite/assisting side, and then move the hands together so the outstretched fingers are just in front of your nose but just below eye level.

Visualization:

Bright blue light outlined by radiant green

Chapter One Hundred Eighteen: The Eagle

x
x
o
o
x
o
o

Receiving the Eagle indicates that you will soar to the heights, attain a certain amount of fame and recognition and be in the limelight or public view in relation to this question at the time indicated by where you get this sign in the series of seven oracles. Still, this is generally a good sign (unless you are an extreme introvert) and does indicate progress toward the success of your goal. This is especially true if you receive this as the child, the last oracle of the series of seven, for this indicates great success, perhaps a good deal greater than you imagined.

If you receive this oracle before the child, the final oracle, then it may very well be an indication that you need to promote what it is you are striving toward. In this case, advertising may be of help. You need to get the word out. You may even consider writing out what you desire or creating a vision board to make your will clear and to aid the spirits in their endeavors.

The Eagle, however, may also indicate a need to take charge, to direct the efforts toward this goal from above, like a general directing hir army taking an overview of the entire situation and dealing fluidly with every contingency that develops. Looking at this quest overall, what is needed to move it along?

Mantra:

Fosdas alt

Pronounced: Foe-ss – dace ale-t

Meaning: Flying high

Mudra:

Begin with the dominant hand in mudra six and the assisting hand in mudra five. Have the assisting hand across the body near the lower ribs, with the outstretched fingers pointing to opposite side but not extending beyond the body, palm to body. Have the dominant hand with elbow bent, outstretched fingers upward, palm forward. Keeping the assisting hand in place, bring the dominant hand forward moving it slightly from side to side, until the outstretched fingers are pointing forward and away from the body, the arm near to full extension but the elbow still slightly bent.

Visualization:

Luminous greenish blue light

Chapter One Hundred Nineteen: The Fetch

o
x
o
o
x
x
x

The Fetch is a very handy spirit that can get one what one desires. In receiving the Fetch, the oracle is indicating that such a person will more than likely appear in your life in accordance with where you receive this oracle in the series of seven. This person will be an invaluable aid to you and will further your cause greatly. It is vital, however, that you treat this individual with due respect and that you reward hir efforts generously. SHe may seem to be a servant to you, as sHe goes about fetching what you need, but sHe is not beneath you, nor inferior to you and, in fact, may actually be superior and more powerful than you, for certainly sHe is able to obtain for you what you cannot obtain for yours'elf alone.

This oracle may also be an indication that there is something that needs to be fetched. Something you need to move things along and you will have to find some way of getting it. You might say that you are missing the right tool for the job and it is important for you to obtain this tool for it will make things go a whole lot easier if you do. Otherwise, it is rather like using a screwdriver to do what a hammer is needed for.

Overall, this is not so much a sign of success but of the possibility of success if you can find the right way to proceed.

Things will go a lot more smoothly if you can find the correct path.

If you receive this as the child, the outcome, then it is likely that there is still something you need to do to complete your goal. In that case, don't give up. You are almost there.

Mantra:

Tat shodriïn

Pronounced: Tate show – dry - in

Meaning: As instructed

Mudra:

Position the dominant hand in mudra four and the assisting hand in mudra six. Put both hands with outstretched fingers touching your temples as though you are in the midst of getting a psychic message. Leaving the assisting hand in place, bring the dominant hand down and forward until the arm is at full extension and the outstretched fingers are pointing forward, palm down.

Visualization:

Vibrant purple light outlined by blue light

Chapter One Hundred Twenty: The Doppelganger

o
x
o
o
x
x
o

The Doppelganger is a being that is identical to you in form but is most likely different in essence. You might say that most Elvis impersonators are a kind of doppelganger. The doppelganger also is a sort of spirit form. It is an astral version of you. You might even say it is the prototype that your body is based upon. You may have noticed that human and other bodies are a variation on a theme individuated by experience. The doppelganger is the theme or template for your body.

In getting this oracle, you may be noticing that you can't really be in two places at the same time, which means that you may feel a bit overextended. That there is more to do it seems than you have time to do it all. There is so much happening, and so many calls upon your time, you are uncertain whether you can fulfill all your obligations and if you don't, your quest seems unlikely to be fulfilled.

However, don't panic. That will just make things worse. Instead, concentrate on one thing at a time and complete each project as it comes up. It may appear like it will take forever, but you will get things done in due course and you will succeed if you persevere.

Mantra:

Ver el'na tolec nar sylartu

Pronounced: Veer eel – nah toe – leek nair sill – lair – two

Meaning: In my image and likeness

Mudra:

Put the dominant hand in mudra four and the assisting hand in mudra six. Have both elbows bent and at your sides, forearms at a ninety degree angle to body, hands crossed at wrists, dominant wrist topmost, palm downward, outstretched fingers pointing at an angle just off center at front. Move both hands slowly apart toward their respective sides and then as the hands get just beyond the line of the body on each side, flip the hands over so the palms are upward.

Visualization:

Bright violet light outlined by blue light

Chapter One Hundred Twenty-One: The Wizard

x
x
o
o
x
x
x

Getting the Wizard is a blessing for you and the question you have put to the oracles. It certainly indicates your ability to achieve what you desire. It also denotes the development of knowledge, skill and mastery. Be the wizard that you are, let your excellence shine forth and proceed toward the fulfillment of your question. You have what it takes and if you use your skills you will certainly fulfill your desire.

However, if your question is about relationship, there is some indication of needing to find the right person. Only certain special individuals will be able to provide what it is you truly need. If you are pursuing someone who is not also a wizard/wizardress, not another creative genius of some sort, not another elfin fae being, you are wasting your time. It is not that you can't get together with such a person, but that in time you will surely regret it. Right company is very important with this oracle. Making the right connections will further you greatly.

On the other hand, if your question concerns finances or your spiritual path, this is a positive sign, although the admonition about right company and the right connections still applies.

Mantra:

Ralt eldroli murgrijfelïn

Pronounced: Ray-lt eel – drow (rhymes with row) – lie muir gryj (like cry with a 'j') – feel - in

Meaning: Great powers unleashed

Mudra:

Start with the dominant hand in mudra four and the assisting hand in mudra five. Have the assisting hand down and slightly out to the side, palm toward body and the dominant hand straight out from the shoulder to the side, palm downward. Circle the dominant hand three times counterclockwise and then move it down and across the body while the assisting hand comes up to meet it. Bring them together just below rib level to the front of the body, until their wrists meet, the dominant hand palm downward and the assisting hand palm upward.

Visualization:

Luminous purple light outlined with bright green

Chapter One Hundred Twenty-Two: The Witch

x
x
o
o
x
x
o

In getting the Witch among the seven oracles, it is suggested that you do a bit of magic to move things along. If you need to do it alone, that is, of course, okay but it is better if you have others who can join you in this magic. It doesn't have to be complicated. It can be something as simple as drawing a tarot card each day and chanting a spell with it (see our book the Elven Book of Powers). Better yet, if you can get others to join you in doing the Mantra and Mudra series that you received from the formulation of the oracles this would increase your potentiality for success greatly.

The important thing here, however, is to make this magic as natural as possible, as easy as possible, and if possible, even a bit of fun. You can do it while listening to your favorite music, or even while you watch your favorite television show, particularly if it is a show about magic.

This is certainly a good sign to get. A sign that indicates that progress is possible with just a bit of extra effort, done in a way that is not exhausting of your energy but actually revitalizing. If you are straining, you aren't quite doing it right. And don't worry about mistakes. Just keep practicing and you will get it right.

Mantra:

La tägli erst elfro

Pronounced: Lah tag – lie ear-st (rhymes with pierced) eel - fro

Meaning: By names most sacred

Mudra:

Position the dominant hand in mudra four and the assisting hand in mudra five. Have the dominant hand palm down across and against your chest. Have the assisting hand down by your side, palm toward body. Keeping the assisting hand in place, move the dominant hand outward and downward toward its own side so that as it does so the palm turns upward, and then circle it around to its original position. When it is back in place, bring the assisting hand up and position it under the dominant hand, against the body and palm also down.

Visualization:

Bright violet light outlined with vivid green

Chapter One Hundred Twenty-Three: The Robin

o
o
x
x
o
o
x

When you get the Robin, it is an indication that there are only small things that you can do to move things toward your goal. Don't let this frustrate you, however, for the Robin is generally a symbol of new beginnings and new beginnings are often slow at first and a bit of caution is advised. Don't rush things, don't attempt to move things faster than they are going; do what the situation requires of you and let things develop mostly on their own. The times will gradually change and movement may very well quicken later, but for now be content with slow success, for at least you are moving toward your goal and that is what is really important.

The Robin is noted for establishing its territory through the use of song. Rather a battle of the bands kind of thing (see Emma Bull's great novel of the Faerie folk the War for the Oaks). So it may happen that you will also have to establish your territory, your right to proceed toward your goal. You may be challenged by another, but let your response be logical and reasonable and a matter of superior oratory or communication. Don't let it devolve into a physical confrontation. If you do, you have lost, even if you seem to win. This is a matter of superior charm and intelligence, not superior strength.

Mantra:

Noc la noc

Pronounced: Nock lah nock

Meaning: Bit by bit

Mudra:

Have the dominant hand in mudra seven and the assisting hand in mudra two. Have both hands in front of you, elbows bent at sides, forearms at forty-five degree angle to body, outstretched fingers of the assisting hand resting between the fingers of the dominant hand, palms toward belly. Now bring the assisting hand up to its shoulder, palm facing across the front of body to opposite side, while the assisting hand goes forward with outstretched fingers pointing away from you and palm downward.

Visualization:

Radiant reddish amber light

Chapter One Hundred Twenty-Four: The Snake

o
o
x
x
o
o
o

The Snake is noted for being a coldblooded creature that sheds its skin. It is traditionally a symbol of knowledge, particularly esoteric and arcane knowledge, and sometimes wisdom. It is sometimes said that the story of St. Patrick driving the snakes out of Ireland really refers to his overcoming and driving out the Druids, who were the knowledgeable ones. In obtaining this oracle, it is an indication that technique and knowledge, rather than emotion in this case, is the key to success.

Also, because the snake sheds its skin there is an indication that you may have to change yours'elf or the way you are approaching this issue. Note that when a snake sheds its skin, it isn't changing its essence or inner being; it is merely transforming the way it appears to the world. So you may also need to polish up your aura and your personality to move things toward your goal.

If you receive this as the final oracle, the child, it is an indication that you may change upon achieving your goal. This is, again, not likely to be a thorough or deep transformation, but rather a change of the way you interact with the world, perhaps an alteration of scene or social circle.

Mantra:

La catyl mamosva

Pronounced: Lah cah – till may – moe-ss - vah

Meaning: By cunning efficiency

Mudra:

Place the dominant hand in mudra seven and the assisting hand in mudra two. Have the dominant hand at opposite shoulder, palm toward body. Have the assisting hand so the outstretched fingers are up pointing upward toward sky/ceiling and are between your eyes in front of your face, palm toward opposite side. Keeping the dominant hand in place, move the assisting hand outward to about a forty-five degree angle and back twice, then across to opposite shoulder, palm to shoulder, then forward and out to full extension of your arm, outstretched fingers pointing forward and away from you, and palm toward opposite side.

Visualization:

Brilliant amber light outlined by bright red

Chapter One Hundred Twenty-Five: Elfin

o
x
o
x
o
x
x

Receiving this oracle among the seven is a great sign no matter where you get it. If you obtain it among the grandparents then it is a sign that progress toward your goal will move along swiftly and completion achieved fairly quickly. There should be rapid progress toward success. If you receive it as one of the parents then, depending on the grandparents that came before it, it indicates that even if things had been slow or blocked at first, that things would begin to move more easily toward the desired outcome. In the place of the outcome or the child, it is indicative of a very successful conclusion quite possibly occurring very suddenly.

This is a very lucky oracle to receive, however, there is a caveat that attends it and that is that one must continue to work on and maintain the success one achieves. It is rather like romance, courtship and marriage really. It is not enough to romance your intended and marry hir, if the marriage is to be a success one must continually strive to make it so. So, too, in obtaining this oracle, you need to remember that this success is to be nurtured and that victory brings responsibility. If you attend to what needs to be done, then all will go well into the future bringing you greater success still.

Mantra:

Ena weya murvylfådas

Pronounced: E – nah we – yah muir – vill – fah - dace

Meaning: With attention unwavering

Mudra:

Start with the dominant hand in mudra three and the assisting hand in mudra six. Have the assisting hand across body and pointing toward opposite hip, palm to body. Have the dominant hand across body to opposite shoulder, palm downward. Leaving the assisting hand in place, move the dominant hand out and across body to its own side until the arm is at full extension out from its shoulder, palm downward. Keeping the elbow out and extended away from body, loop the hand and forearm around so that when it returns to full extension the palm is forward.

Visualization:

Luminous orange light outlined by radiant blue

Chapter One Hundred Twenty-Six: Faerie

o
x
o
x
o
x
o

Getting Faerie indicates good luck and blessings upon you and toward a positive outcome of the question you have put to the oracles. However, getting Faerie also indicates a need for a little greater concentration, focus and seriousness toward this goal, especially if you get this as one of the grandparents. If you receive this as the outcome, the child, then your wish will surely be achieved but there is a caution to this: use what you have accomplished well. Do the most and make the most of what you have achieved or what has come to you.

Be of good cheer, wherever this oracle comes to you in the unfolding of the seven, the Light of Faerie shines upon you and this will certainly bring luck into your life and quite possibly unexpected rewards that will brighten your life but which were not a direct part of your question and will most likely appear in a surprising way. There is a sort of bonus to receiving Faerie.

With the wings of a faerie you may soar above obstacles, but remember to flap your wings. Flying takes a bit of effort.

Mantra:

Varigos låka

Pronounced: Vair (rhymes with hair) – rye - goes lah - kay

Meaning: Forever after

Mudra:

Position the dominant hand in mudra three and the assisting hand in mudra six. Have both hands forward and crossed at wrists, assisting hand over dominant hand, palms downward. Keeping the wrists together, bring both hands to chest so outstretched fingers are pointing upward and off to opposite sides, palms toward chest and the dominant hand is in front of assisting hand, which is to say farther away from the body. Keeping the assisting hand in place, move the dominant hand forward and out so the outstretched fingers are now pointing away from the body and the palm is toward opposite side.

Visualization:

Vivid orange light outlined by light blue

Chapter One Hundred Twenty-Seven: The Elven Star

x

o

x

o

x

o

x

The seven pointed acute angled star of the Elven people, sometimes called the Faerie star, is a sign of tremendous luck and a very fortunate indication of success for the question you have put to the oracles. However, there is a small caveat with it and that is don't screw it up. You are pretty much guaranteed to succeed concerning this question, no matter where you receive this among the seven oracles, as long as you don't do anything to obstruct yours'elf and the fulfillment of this wish. Getting the Elven Star indicates that you just need to get out of your own way and let your spirit and your soul shine forth and all that you desire will come to you.

If you use this luck and blessing to help your others, your elfin faerie kindred, then you will be doubly blessed and triply blest.

Mantra:

Murted vorundur

Pronounced: Muir – teed vor – rune - dur

Meaning: Until completion

Mudra:

Begin with the dominant hand in mudra six and the assisting hand in mudra three. Have the assisting arm at full extension out from the shoulder, palm downward. Have the dominant hand across body, elbow up, outstretched fingers pointing along the line of the assisting arm, palm downward. Keeping the dominant hand in place, bring the assisting hand in to settle just beyond the opposite side cheek, palm toward cheek, outstretched fingers pointing upward and backward at an angle.

Visualization:

Bright blue light outlined by vibrant orange light

Chapter One Hundred Twenty-Eight: The Faerie Star

x
o
x
o
x
o
o

The Faerie Star is exactly the same as the Elven Star and bears the same luck with it, except the Faeries saw our elven star and changed its name to suit them. Therefore, in obtaining this oracle among the seven, it is a sign that you should take all that you encounter and make it your own. Make the world work for you, so to speak. Take everything that you like and everything that moves and inspires you and translate it into your own view and perspective of the world, life and the Universe. Individualize your path. Individualize your magic.

In receiving this oracle, you are advised to be adaptable and flexible and ever ready to change and transform to create a better s'elf, a more successful and perfect version of yours'elf. All that you encounter can be turned toward your advantage. This is one of the secrets of elfae (elven and faerie) magic. If you can do that then you are not only blest but you are powerful beyond imagining. But don't forget those who inspired you and always give credit where credit is due, which is another way of acknowledging and remembering the ancestral spirits. Wherever it occurs in the series of seven, this oracle is a sign that your wish will surely be achieved but you may wish to dress up for the occasion.

Mantra:

Va tay lefa zed

Pronounced: Vah tay lee-fah zeed

Meaning: To the very end

Mudra:

Place the dominant hand in mudra six and the assisting hand in mudra three. Have both hands down at sides, palms toward body. Bring the dominant hand up until it is resting and pointing toward the opposite shoulder, palm toward body. Bring the assisting hand up so that it is pointing to the opposite shoulder, wrist crossed over the wrist of the dominant hand. Keeping the dominant hand in place, bring the assisting hand back down to its side, palm toward rear. Now, bring the dominant hand down to its side, palm also to rear. Then bring the assisting hand back up and pointing toward opposite shoulder again, and then do the same with the dominant hand, only this time the dominant wrist will be in front of, that is to say farther away from the body, crossed over the assisting wrist. Now, bring both hands back down to their respective sides and slightly out from the body with palms to front.

Visualization:

Luminous blue light outlined by light orange

"The path to Elfin is only straight and narrow for brief periods, most of the time it is as convoluted as a deer trail through the forest."

—Wisdom of the Silver Elves

Appendix A

Mudra One

Index and middle finger outstretched, ring and pinkie fingers turned in, thumb over them.

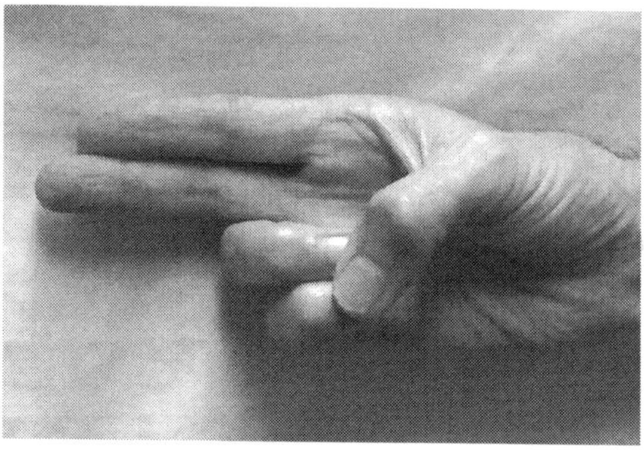

Mudra Two

Index, middle and ring fingers outstretched, pinkie turned in, thumb over pinkie.

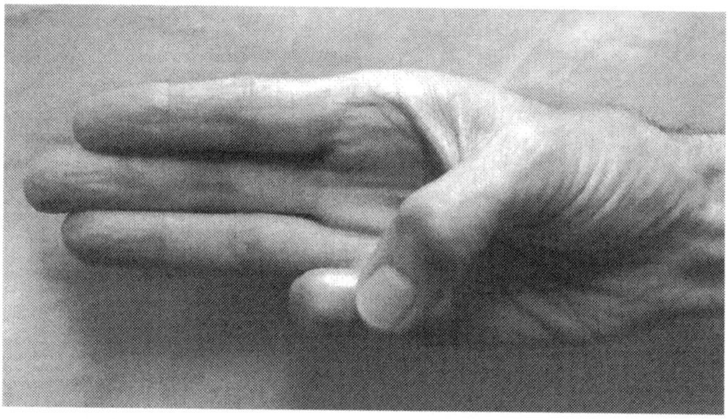

Mudra Three

Index finger turned inward, thumb over it, middle, ring and pinkie fingers outstretched.

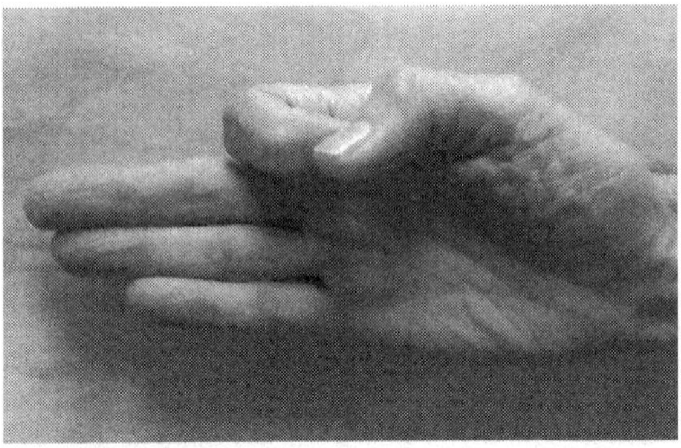

Mudra Four

Middle finger turned in, thumb over it, index, ring and pinkie outstretched.

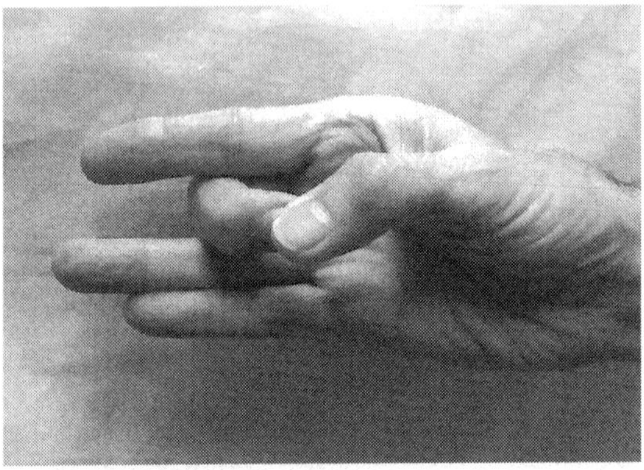

Mudra Five

Index, middle and pinkie outstretched, ring finger turned inward, thumb upon it.

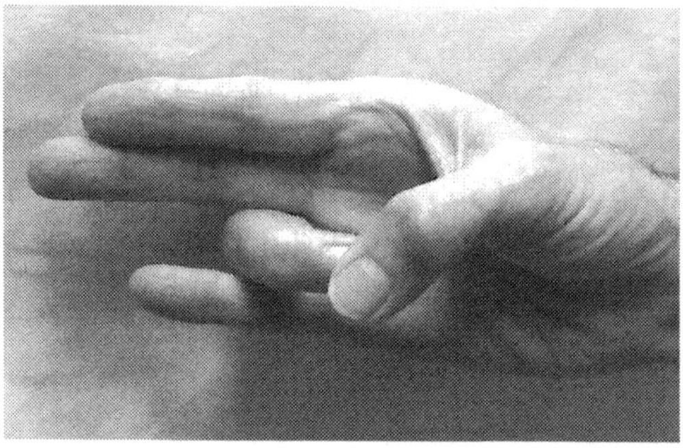

Mudra Six

Index and pinkie outstretched, middle and ring finger folded in, thumb restraining them.

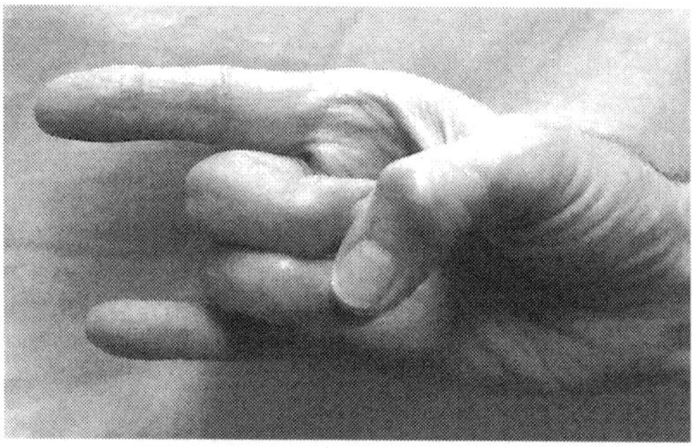

Mudra Seven

A closed fist with thumb over fingers.

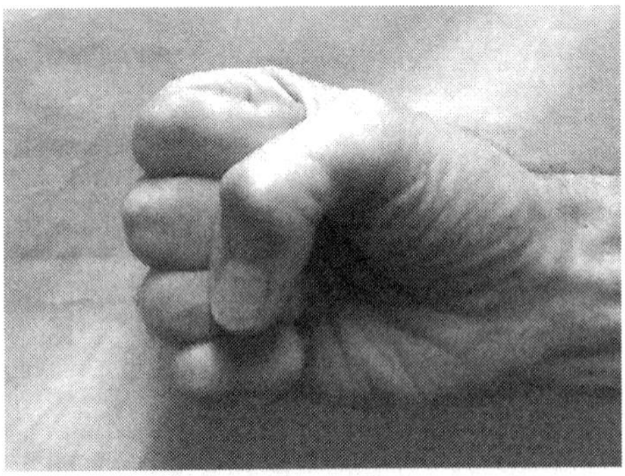

Mudra Eight

An open hand, all fingers outstretched including thumb in what is known in martial arts as a spear hand.

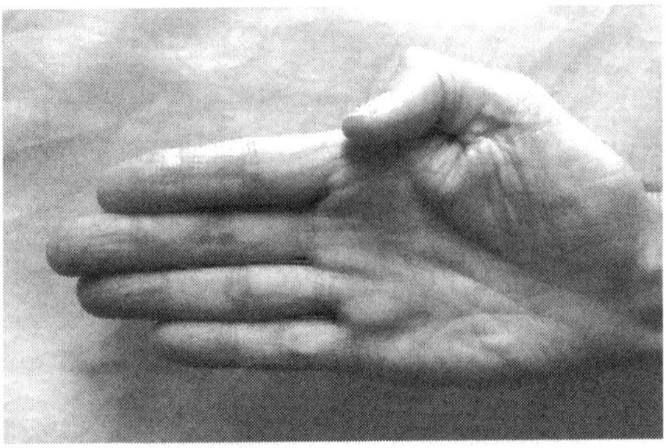

Appendix B

If the bottom most figure of your oracle is X or an odd number, consult **Table 1** on page 260. If it is O or an even number, consult **Table 2** on page 261. The left side of the chart is the lower four figures, the top is the upper three. The numbers are the chapter numbers. Use this reference for finding your oracles quickly and easily.

Table 1 **Top 3 ➔** **Lower 4 🡇**	X X X	O O X	O X O	X O O	O O O	X X O	X O X	O X X
X X X X	1	67	9	51	21	17	27	85
O O X X	49	101	5	53	47	83	41	33
O X O X	11	79	57	7	13	117	127	93
X O O X	65	123	77	103	29	105	111	61
O O O X	23	31	15	45	3	39	69	
X X O X	87	63	95	35	91	113	99	55
X O X X	25	109	125	43	71	73	59	97
O X X X	19	107	119	81	37	121	75	115

Table 2 **Top 3 ➔** **Lower 4 ➔**	X X X	O O X	O X O	X O O	O O O	X X O	X O X	O X X
X X X O	4	68	10	52	22	18	28	86
O O X O	50	102	6	54	48	84	42	34
O X O O	12	80	58	8	14	118	128	94
X O O O	66	124	78	104	30	106	112	62
O O O O	24	32	16	46	2	40	70	90
X X O O	88	64	96	36	92	114	100	56
X O X O	26	110	126	44	72	74	60	98
O X X O	20	108	120	82	38	122	76	116

About the Authors

The Silver Elves The Silver Elves, Zardoa and Silver Flame, are a family of elves who have been living and sharing the Elven Way since 1975. They are the authors of 39 books on magic and enchantment, available on Amazon, and your local bookstore, including:

The Book of Elven Runes: A Passage Into Faerie;

The Magical Elven Love Letters, volume I, 2, and 3;

An Elfin Book of Spirits: Evoking the Beneficent Powers of Faerie;

Caressed by an Elfin Breeze: The Poems of Zardoa Silverstar;

Eldafaryn: True Tales of Magic from the Lives of the Silver Elves;

Arvyndase (Silverspeech): A Short Course in the Magical Language of the Silver Elves;

The Elven Book of Dreams: A Magical Oracle of Faerie;

The Book of Elven Magick: The Philosophy and Enchantments of the Seelie Elves, Volume 1 & 2;

What An Elf Would Do: A Magical Guide to the Manners and Etiquette of the Faerie Folk;

The Elven Tree of Life Eternal: A Magical Quest for One's True S'Elf;

Magic Talks: On Being a Correspondence Between the Silver Elves and the Elf Queen's Daughters;

Sorcerers' Dialogues: A Further Correspondence Between the Silver Elves and the Founders of the Elf Queen's Daughters;

Discourses on High Sorcery: More Correspondence Between the Silver Elves and the Founders of the Elf Queen's Daughters;

Ruminations on Necromancy: Continuing Correspondence Between the Silver Elves and the Founders of the Elf Queen's Daughter;

The Elven Way: The Magical Path of the Shining Ones;

The Book of Elf Names: 5,600 Elven Names to Use for Magic, Game Playing, Inspiration, Naming One's Self and One's Child, and as Words in the Elven Language of the Silver Elves;

Elven Silver: The Irreverent Faery Tales of Zardoa Silverstar;

An Elven Book of Ryhmes: Book Two of the Magical Poems of Zardoa Silverstar;

The Voice of Faerie: Making Any Tarot Deck Into an Elven Oracle;

Liber Aelph: Words of Guidance from the Silver Elves to our Magical Children;

The Shining Ones: The Elfin Spirits That Guide You According to Your Birth Date and the Evolutionary Lessons They Offer;

Living the Personal Myth: Making the Magic of Faerie Real in One's Own Personal Life;

Elf Magic Mail, The Original Letters of the Elf Queen's Daughters with Comentary by the Silver Elves, Book 1 and 2;

The Elves of Lyndarys: A Magical Tale of Modern Faerie Folk;

The Elf Folk's Book of Cookery: Recipes For a Delighted Tongue, a Healthy Body and a Magical Life;

Faerie Unfolding: The Cosmic Expression of the Divine Magic;

The Elements of Elven Magic: A New View of Calling the Elementals Based Upon the Periodic Table of Elements;

The Keys to Elfin Enchantment: Mastery of the Faerie Light Through the Portals of Manifestation;

Elf Quotes: A Collection of Over 1000 Ancient Elven Sayings and Wise Elfin Koans by The Silver Elves About Magic and The Elven Way; and

The United States of Elfin Imagining A More Elven Style of Government.

The Silver Elves have had various articles published in *Circle Network News Magazine* since 1986 and have given out over

6,000 elven names to interested individuals in the Arvyndase language, with each elf name having a unique meaning specifically for that person. They are also mentioned numerous times in *Not In Kansas Anymore* by Christine Wicker (Harper San Francisco, 2005), *A Field Guide to Otherkin* by Lupa (Megalithica Books, 2007), and Nikolay Laypanenko's recent book *The Elves From Ancient Times To Our Days: The Magical Heritage of "Starry People" and their Continuation Into the Modern World* (2017) that gives a detailed account of our involvement in the Elven Movement since 1975. Also, an interview with the Silver Elves is included in Emily Carding's recent book *Faery Craft* (Llewellyn Publications, 2012*)*.

The Silver Elves understand the world as a magical or miraculous phenomena, and that all beings, by pursuing their own true path, will become whomever they truly desire to be. You are welcome to visit their website at http://silverelves.angelfire.com and join them on Facebook with the names as "Michael J. Love (Silver Elves)" and "Martha Char Love (Silver Flame)."

20396268R00154

Printed in Great Britain
by Amazon